Fables of Fact

John Hellmann

FABLES OF FACT

The New Journalism
as New Fiction

UNIVERSITY OF ILLINOIS PRESS

Urbana   Chicago   London

Library of Congress Cataloging in Publication Data

Hellmann, John, 1948–
    Fables of fact.
    Bibliography: p.
    Includes index.
    1. American prose literature—20th century—History
and criticism. 2. Journalism—United States.
    3. Fiction—Technique. I. Title.
PS369.H44   813'.081'09   80–23881
ISBN 0–252–00847–2

To Marilyn

Contents

Preface

From the debate set off by the publication of Truman Capote's *In Cold Blood* in 1965 to the Pulitzer Prize for fiction awarded to Norman Mailer's *Executioner's Song* in 1979, the combining of literary technique and journalistic fact has developed into an important, if still widely misunderstood, response to the dislocations of contemporary American experience. While a number of works in this form, most commonly called the "new journalism" or the "nonfiction novel," have gained wide recognition as contemporary classics, most of them have nevertheless received remarkably little analysis and elucidation, with major questions about the genre as a whole remaining insufficiently explored. Far too many of the articles and essays on the topic have been content to make general observations about the use of fictive techniques in journalistic narrative, or to debate endlessly the apparent paradox in the term "nonfiction novel," or to focus on the legitimacy (or lack thereof) of the word "new" in "new journalism."

Other than collections of essays or source materials, three major studies of the genre have thus far appeared. As the earliest, Michael Johnson's *New Journalism: The Underground Press, the Artists of Nonfiction, and Changes in the Established Media* (1971) was a well-researched and considered introduction to the topic. But because Johnson includes within his subject all innovative developments in journalism during the 1960's, from counterculture magazines to advocacy journalism to precision journalism, the specific literary genre that the term "new journalism" usually describes receives necessarily limited attention in a single chapter. John Hollowell's *Fact and Fiction: The New Journalism and the Nonfiction Novel* (1977) and Mas'ud Zavarzadeh's *Mythopoeic Reality: The Postwar American Nonfiction Novel* (1976) are the only books heretofore devoted completely to a study of the form as literature. Hollowell's book serves as a readable, well-organized survey of the topic, but relies heavily on Tom Wolfe's identification of the central importance of certain techniques of journalism and realistic fiction as the basis of his critical approach—an emphasis that I think is misleading. Zavarzadeh's *Mythopoeic Reality*, by contrast, is a highly theoretical and complex work that focuses upon the nonfiction novel in order to make major points about contemporary reality and narrative. In his discussion of the fictive quality of contemporary experience, in the profound questions he raises, and in his consideration of the nonfiction novel as an experimental literature, Zavarzadeh is provocative and has had a significant influence on the present study. But I am in disagreement with his central thesis—that the nonfiction novelists consistently seek merely to transcribe actuality in order to reveal absurdity, and that in writing this nonfiction they avoid the "totalizing" function of the modern novelists in order to work more like the French new novelists.

I propose the present study, then, as a *reconsideration* of a body of writing in our contemporary literature, a reconsideration both of the significance and of the nature of that writing. Unlike those guardians of tradition who have ignored the genre because of its claims to newness and its merging of long-standing distinctions, and the exponents of the avant-garde who have suspected the form because of its popularity and presumed topicality, I have tried to evaluate new journalism on its own merits and to observe its actual characteristics. That process has led me to a view of new journalism different in its central points from the more commonly held attitudes and previously developed theories.

In this study I attempt to show that new journalistic works, far from being realistically dramatized documentaries or even absurdist transcriptions of fact, are profoundly *transforming* literary experiments embodying confrontations between fact and mind, between the worlds of journalism and fiction. Their authors attempt to "make up" or construct meaningful versions of the "news" that continually threatens to overwhelm consciousness. And the major artists of the genre have done so, not by merely reporting facts through scenic description and dramatic dialogue or by tape recording actual events, but by combining the unique credibility of journalism with the self-reflexive pattern-making of fabulist fiction. The result is a form of journalism which, in its most essential methods and concerns, is a genre of the new fiction; it deals with fact through fable, discovering, constructing, and self-consciously exploring meaning beyond our media-constructed "reality," our "news."

In making this reconsideration I have aimed at combining overview with close analysis. In Chapter I I discuss new journalism in the contexts of both conventional American journalism and realistic fiction, and explain how it has developed along with fabulist fiction as a reaction against the weaknesses of both in the face of an altered "reality." In Chapter II I attempt to show why the form should be approached as primarily literature—indeed, as a genre of fiction—despite its adherence to the factual criteria of journalism. I have then chosen four major authors of new journalism, Norman Mailer, Hunter S. Thompson, Tom Wolfe, and Michael Herr, for individual study in separate chapters. While seeking to avoid an overly schematized approach, I have in each chapter discussed an author's individual approach to the form as he uniquely combines a journalistic subject with certain fabulist techniques; I have then attempted a close analysis of that approach as it is embodied in one or more major works. In this way I have tried to maintain focus while achieving a measure of fullness. It is my hope that this study will lead to a more complete understanding of the achievement of the authors working in new journalism, and to a reconsideration of the significance of the form to contemporary American literature and society.

This study has benefited at various stages from the generous help of others. Wayne Kvam in particular provided invaluable criticism of the early draft. Anthony Libby, Stanley Gontarski, Carl Moore, Ottavio Casale, Robert Bamberg, Yoshinobu Hakutani, Michael Lennon, William Sullivan, Julian Markels, and John Muste also made helpful suggestions. The English Department of Kent State University awarded me a Pringle Fellowship during 1976-77, which allowed me to devote myself to beginning this study relatively free of distraction. Ann Lowry Weir of the University of Illinois Press provided skilled guidance in the preparation of the final version of the manuscript. Sally Saxe and Judy Von Blon expertly and patiently typed it. My wife Marilyn, with both her criticism and her confidence, was of incalculable help. Finally, I take this opportunity to thank my parents for their unfailing support.

Various sections of this book have previously appeared, in most cases in considerably different form, in the following journals: *The Centennial Review, Critique, Adena, The South Atlantic Quarterly* and *Genre.* I thank the editors of those publications for giving me my first opportunities to present my ideas on the new journalism.

1

Introduction: Fact, Fable, and the New Journalist

The terms "new journalism" and "nonfiction novel" both serve as names for a contemporary genre in which journalistic material is presented in the forms of fiction. While there are a number of precedents extending back through the history of both journalism and prose fiction, the beginning of the new journalism and the nonfiction novel (at least as a discernible form or movement) can with some symbolic justification be dated as 1965, the year when Tom Wolfe's *Kandy-Kolored Tangerine-Flake Streamline Baby* and Truman Capote's *In Cold Blood* were published. *Kandy-Kolored* was Wolfe's first collection, and in its preface he fueled the debate over a "new journalism" by asserting that the genesis of his unorthodox approach lay in a need to go beyond the limitations of conventional journalism. Capote likewise launched considerable debate in literary circles with the publication of *In Cold Blood* and his well-published claims that it was the first work of a new literary genre. The term "new journalism" that became associated with Wolfe's work, and the term "nonfiction novel" used by Capote, in themselves stimulated a controversy that was often more fierce than perceptive; still, it contributed to recognition of the form as a vital new force in contemporary American society. While the two terms may be used to describe the same works, they indicate the separate origins of this form of writing. Wolfe improvised his new journalism out of a frustration experienced while working within the limits of newspaper conventions; Capote calculatingly developed his nonfiction novel from a long-entertained theory to a new chapter in his literary career. Yet it must be considered more than a coincidence that Wolfe and Capote developed the forms simultaneously, for they were only the most visible experiments in a genre responding to a unique shift in American culture.

With the beginning of the 1960's, American reality was undergoing a profound transformation. Stimulated by Kennedy's election and unleashed by his assassination, long-buried forces in the American psyche were coming to the surface with an almost eerie simultaneity in politics, in national and individual violence, in subcultures, in urban slums, in technology, in the young. Mass-media journalism was now present as an added force, making its versions of these events part of the national consciousness. The individual American found himself daily confronted by realities that were as actual as they seemed fictive (a quality inherent partly in the events, and partly in the fact that television presented them in formulas of simple conflict and melodramatic action drawn from its fictional entertainments). Both novelists and reporters found themselves faced with situations demanding responses, situations for which they soon realized their tools were inadequate. A significant number turned to the form that is the subject of this book. Before the publication of *Kandy-Kolored* and *In Cold Blood*, Norman Mailer had already written startling accounts of Kennedy's nomination at the Democratic convention in Los Angeles, and of the Liston-Patterson heavyweight championship fight. Hunter S. Thompson was publishing parts of his adventures with the Hell's Angels motorcycle gang in *The Nation*. Jimmy Breslin, George Plimpton, Joan Didion, and Gay Talese were all experimenting with the form (Talese's articles had been an early influence on Wolfe). Michael Herr would soon be going to Vietnam to observe and write. Working separately, novelists and reporters were moving toward each others' forms in order to better confront a new set of American realities.

Since the mass media were so essential a part of the new situation, I will first consider their role, the problems involving them, and the resulting move away from their forms made by the young writers who came to be called new journalists. Living and writing in the 1960's, reporters such as Wolfe, Thompson, and Herr found themselves saddled with rules and formulas that made it impossible for them to deal adequately with their subjects. As Nicolaus Mills has stated in the preface to his anthology of new journalistic writing: "A who, what, where, when, why style of reporting could not begin to capture the anger of a black power movement or the euphoria of a Woodstock." [1] Confronted by subjects the significance of which lay in their experience, in their *consciousness*, many journalists found that conventional reporting only made the subjects seem stranger. They revolted against such rigid forms as the "inverted pyramid" (in which isolated facts are presented in declining order of importance), and the "on the one hand . . . on the other hand" news analysis. They also rejected conventional journalism's assumed perspective of "objectivity" and its reliance on official, often concealed, sources. Instead, they sought new forms and frankly asserted their personal perspectives.

Detractors of new journalism often assume that it is a hybrid form that mixes the content of fiction (read: falsehood) with that of journalism (read: truth). Actually, the new journalists seek to merge the sophisticated and fluid forms provided by fiction with the facts sought in journalism. As Gay Talese asserts in the preface to *Fame and Obscurity*, a collection of his new journalistic work, "the new journalism, though reading like fiction, is not fiction. It is, or should be, as reliable as the most reliable reportage although it seeks a larger truth. . . ." [2] The phrase "a larger truth" is a key statement of the need that caused new journalists to abandon the limitations of conventional journalism. The contemporary individual was in less need of facts than of an understanding of the facts already available. Wolfe has likewise emphasized his desire to communicate the *experience* and *meaning* of his subjects in their full ambiguities and complexities, through the use of such fictional devices as construction of scenes, dialogue, interior point of view, and the recording of significant details of dress and milieu. Likewise, in opposition to the mass media's convention of objectivity, he has emphasized the importance the new journalist places on going to the subject and to the work itself with a fresh perspective as free as possible from preconceived ideas and predetermined forms.

Reviewers have often noted this quality in new journalistic works. In his early study, *The New Journalism*, Michael Johnson speaks of how Mailer approaches the Apollo program in *Of a*

Fire on the Moon "with a kind of childlike sense of wonder and openness—a starting point for any really good journalist—which he tempers with moral judgment and esthetic control derived from experience." [3] Similarly, *Newsweek* compared Thompson's writings about the sham of the conventional press's portrayal of presidential campaigns to the attacks on society made by the young Holden Caulfield in J. D. Salinger's classic 1950's novel, *The Catcher in the Rye*.[4] New journalistic works are often patterned in this movement from innocence to experience, as the writer moves past press releases and press agents to penetrate the mysteries behind the appearance. This openness enables the writers to break through the prepackaged insights and perspectives which permeate the corporate fiction produced by conventional journalism.

Admirers of conventional journalism have portrayed the conflict with new journalism as one of objectivity versus subjectivity and fact versus fiction. However, it is actually a conflict of a disguised perspective versus an admitted one, and a corporate fiction versus a personal one. In either case, journalism is necessarily an extension of all human perception and communication in its fictional (that is, shaping) quality. Because it is a product of the human mind and language, journalism can never passively mirror the whole of reality, but must instead actively select, transform, and interpret it. The problem with conventional journalism is that, while it inevitably shares in these limitations (or opportunities), it nevertheless refuses to acknowledge the creative nature of its "news," instead concealing the structuring mechanisms of its organizational mind behind masks of objectivity and fact.

The established print and television media daily create prepackaged fictions of events which become the national reality for Americans. Decades ago Walter Lippmann discussed the tendency of the print media to create and perpetuate "stereotypes," and he worried about the greater power for this distorting process suggested by the advent of film.[5] In recent years Timothy Crouse, in *The Boys on the Bus*, has chronicled the phenomenon of "pack journalism," wherein reporters innocently conspire to create a uniform version of a presidential campaign, rather than to present their individual perceptions of it.[6] In *News from*

Nowhere Edward Epstein has made a similarly probing analysis of network television's claim to "mirror" reality, delineating in carefully illustrated and documented detail the political, economic, organizational, and technical forces which constitute a "web of expectations" determining the shape of the "story," regardless of the event's true significance.[7] The televised fiction has become so powerful that the supposedly first-hand fictions of the print media sometimes even use it as their unacknowledged subject matter. Consider this account of the 1976 Republican convention in Kansas City from the *National Village Voice:*

Industrious reporters at these conventions now sit with small TV sets in front of them, glancing up and down from the screen to the actual events occurring before their eyes like chickens undecided where the better drink is coming from. The better equipped then type their stories on one of those modern electronic machines also furnished with a screen. This is not to ridicule such practices—almost the only way of finding out what is going on generally and of transmitting it rapidly to the readers—but it does explain why many of the news stories tend to look the same: Everyone is hooked into the same electro-actual reality.[8]

We have been disoriented not merely by the surreal events of contemporary life—"live" assassinations, Tet, Woodstock, moon walks, Watergate, the SLA's televised "last stand," Gary Gilmore's execution, the Jonestown mass suicide—but by the insufficiently explained, unfelt, and anonymously formulated versions of them which the conventional media provide. Because of the nature of human cognition and communication, symbolic images of events, rather than the events themselves, are all we can ever know. Unfortunately, conventional journalism reinforces and multiplies the problems of this process through disguised perspective and rigid formula. As a result, mass media confront the individual with a national news comprised of distorted images and short-circuiting information, while failing to offer the individual a meaningful relation to it.

A closely related problem is the corporate media's reluctance to admit their role in the events they witness. In the early 1960's Daniel Boorstin was already emphasizing how much of our "reality" now consists of "pseudo-events" manufactured for and by the media.[9] In the same decade this influence became a political issue, as the press was accused of consciously and unconsciously fueling riots. In recent years television's participation in events has grown so obvious that it has drawn the attention even of the corporate print media. Consider this *Time* account of the situation at the 1976 Democratic convention in New York City:

Some of the week's most unusual convention action may come when the dozen network floor reporters—accompanied by cameramen, relief correspondents and producers—slug it out with 3,000 other journalists and 5,000 delegates and alternates for breathing space on the claustrophobic Madison Square Garden floor (30,000 sq. ft., or about half the size of a football field). "There might be a few ripped trousers and coats. There might be a few bumps and bruises," says NBC's Pettit. Of course, some kind of action like that may be necessary to keep the nomination of a presidential candidate from being upstaged by *Bionic Woman*.[10]

Yet television cameras and microphones are only the most obvious aspects of media participation in, and thus alteration of, an event. Modern quantum physics has shown that even the most delicate instrument of observation necessarily alters the phenomenon observed. The same is true for any reporter, no matter how unobtrusive he may be. To ignore this through the conventions of "objective" narration is to deny part of the reality of the event observed.

This tendency of the media not only to fail to reckon with the new realities of American society, but actually to further distort them is a major problem for an American trying to comprehend his "global village." In fact, the need to break through the media-created corporate fiction is one of the major motivations and themes of new journalistic works. Tom Wolfe, for instance, first created his unique art in an act of humiliating struggle with conventional ideas and forms. Assigned to write a story on a Hot Rod & Custom Car show for the *Herald Tribune*, he wrote the superficial and condescending feature generally granted to such subjects. The problem, he says, was not even with the paper's forms, but with himself: the subject was simply "outside the system of ideas I was used to working with, even though I had been through the whole Ph.D. route at Yale, in American Studies and everything." [11] Moreover, when he later researched the subject anew for *Esquire*, he found that he could not pull his materials together into the traditional magazine feature; instead he had to type them up in a memorandum for managing editor Byron Dobell, who then planned to turn the story over to another writer. Once Dobell had read the memorandum, which was typed up in the form of a personal letter, he decided simply to delete the "Dear Byron" and run it as it was.[12] Wolfe had found his voice, breaking free from his outmoded academic preconceptions and from rigid journalistic forms.

With this same openness to experience and impulse toward unformulated truth, Hunter S. Thompson launched his career as a new journalist in direct reaction against conventional journalism. *Hell's Angels* was intended to correct the distorted popular image of motorcycle gangs created by both the government and the press. Similarly, after beginning Book I of *The Armies of the Night* with *Time*'s account of his role in the 1967 march on the Pentagon, Norman Mailer moves into his own account by saying, "Now we may leave *Time* in order to find out what happened."[13] In Book II he resumes this theme as he explains the methods by which he hopes to avoid emulating "the mass media which surrounded the March on the Pentagon and created a forest of inaccuracy which would blind the efforts of an historian."[14] And in his writing on Vietnam, Michael Herr asserts that "conventional journalism could no more reveal this war than conventional firepower could win it."[15] He makes it clear that his aim in *Dispatches* is to communicate a deeper subject: "The press got all the facts (more or less), it got too many of them. But it never found a way to report meaningfully about death, which of course was really what it was all about."[16]

The new journalist exploits the transformational resources of human perception and imagination to seek out a fresher and more complete experience of an event, and then to re-create that experience into a personally shaped "fiction" which communicates something approaching the wholeness and resonance it has had for him. Typically, the new journalist approaches his subject matter from the vantage point of a relentless witness and detective (Capote, John Hersey), as an involved participant (Mailer, Thompson, Herr), or from the inside of the subjects themselves (Wolfe, Talese). Above all, the new journalist wishes to use his imaginative powers and fictional craft to seek out and construct meaning. For this reason obtrusive "style" and other signs of a writer's individual perspective are frankly, even assertively, present. Almost by definition, new journalism is a revolt by the individual against homogenized forms of experience, against monolithic versions of truth. Wolfe is certainly correct in stating that new journalism enjoys "only the outlaw's rule regarding technique: take, use, improvise." [17] Only through an openness of idea and form can any truly "new" information be reported; otherwise, a journalist merely places new facts into old formulas. The new journalist seeks not only new facts, but also the new ideas and forms through which they can develop a new meaning, and therefore perhaps approach a truth.

The weaknesses of conventional journalism revealed in the 1960's were one force contributing to the rise of the new journalism. The same situation was making weaknesses in traditional fiction similarly obvious to contemporary novelists. In 1961 Philip Roth, who had launched his promising career with the realistic novella *Goodbye, Columbus*, was already warning of the problems faced by an American writer in simply "trying to understand, and then describe, and then make *credible* much of the American reality." [18] The conventions and techniques of realistic fiction most fully developed during the later nineteenth century did not seem to satisfactorily convey, much less facilitate comprehension of, contemporary experience. Wolfe has claimed that new journalism depends on the use of realistic techniques. In fact, however, he and other new journalists and nonfiction novelists have been far more innovative than that would suggest, for they have had to move beyond the conventions not only of journalism, but of traditional fiction as well. The novelist attempting to set down his world in the early 1960's found that the conventions of realistic writing shared many of the limitations of conventional journalism, since the two were based on similar assumptions about reality. As a result, he became an experimentalist, not out of a theoretical love of the avant-garde, but out of a simple need to find a way to better know and communicate reality.

Because the problems faced by the fiction writer were basic

ones of knowledge and communication, they corresponded closely to those of all individuals in the society. Change and fragmentation had come to substitute for the stable body of "manners and morals"—the sum of beliefs, habits, expectations, codes of dress, gestures and stock phrases; in short, the accepted ways of doing things—that normally characterize a society. American society had always been marked by a relative transience and turmoil; indeed, nineteenth-century authors such as Nathaniel Hawthorne had complained of the lack of the solid culture needed for writing a novel. Because the novel is a form that studies the interaction of individuals within a society, the novelist depends on the reader's knowledge of the culture's pervasive "codes." As we have seen, the forces pushing American society in the 1960's toward change and fragmentation, documented by Alvin Toffler in *Future Shock*, were greatly accelerated by the media. Whereas Hawthorne had found himself facing a dearth of codes, the contemporary novelist found himself confronted by a plethora of lifestyles and subcultures, each with a different set of assumptions and behavior patterns. Moreover, these "societies" were highly unstable: one could not be sure what a certain mode of dress, for instance, signified about the character or class of an individual. An alteration in American reality was perplexing the individual citizen who had to deal with images from Haight-Ashbury, Saigon, the moon, and Washington in rapid succession. That alteration made it difficult for the novelist to use the realistic methods of conventional fiction.

This problem was compounded by the fact that realism was a fictional mode or style—a set of literary conventions and techniques—developed in the nineteenth century to enable the writer to describe the *typical* experience of members of large classes in society. Its proponents had sought to avoid the exotic and inventive, instead preferring the common and representative. The basic assumption of nineteenth-century fiction, like that of twentieth-century journalism, lay in the existence of an objective reality that could be simply recorded. But for most Americans in the 1960's, perhaps the central reality was that everyday life now involved implausible characters and events delivered into the home by the media. The realm of the believable had become an extremely doubtful concept. For a novelist to present either the mundane or the extraordinary through realistic techniques was bound to cause problems of credibility in this situation.

Early American writing, confronted by similar problems in the lack of a stable culture and the presence of strange new realities in the landscape, had turned to the extreme alternatives of romance and factual prose narrative. In the 1960's American fiction writers likewise reacted to a similar (if perhaps more complicated) problem. Although such notable writers as John Updike and Saul Bellow continued to experiment with realist forms, a large group turned away from realism to write fables that clearly made no attempt to represent American life. Typical were Kurt Vonnegut, John Barth, Thomas Pynchon, and Donald Barthelme. Unable to capture American reality through realism, and convinced that America's problems were now too profound for the social and psychological levels that realism most effectively probed, they sought to create autonomous worlds which would indirectly probe and illuminate the actual one. The fable form enabled them to draw on such modes as allegory (in which a narrative is made to develop some philosophical view) and black humor (in which horror is combined with comedy for purposes of psychological defense or expression of absurdity) in order to deal with areas of universal meaning that transcend the chaos of this society. Other fiction writers such as Norman Mailer and Truman Capote moved instead to a direct confrontation with the perplexing reality, drawing on the inherent credibility of factual claims as a partial solution to the writer's dilemma. But, as we have seen, the mere presentation of facts and the use of traditional realistic techniques could not be sufficient. As a result, these writers also adapted and developed innovative techniques similar to those of the fabulists. Using Robert Scholes's term "fabulation" for the new fables, David Lodge was one of the first critics to perceive that the two forms were responses to the same impulse:

The non-fiction novel and fabulation are *radical* forms which take their impetus from an extreme reaction to the world we live in—*The Armies of the Night* and *Giles Goat-Boy* are equally products of the apocalyptic imagination. The assumption behind such experiments is that our "reality" is so extraordinary, horrific or absurd that the methods of conventional realistic imitation are no longer adequate.[19]

New journalism and fabulist fiction are not only creative responses to the same problematic state of realism, but also significantly related approaches to its possible solution. Rejecting the same assumptions and concerns of realistic fiction as no longer tenable, they have for the most part pursued strikingly similar techniques and aims. The major difference between new journalism and contemporary fabulist fiction is one of contract: in both forms the writer contracts an agreement with the reader which frees the former from the need to establish the illusion of reality. In his desire to break through the crisis of credibility in an incredible world, the fiction writer has escaped the problems of plausibility and fragmentation by the radically simple device of assuring the reader that he is dealing in pure fantasy. With just as bold a solution, the new journalist has escaped the same problems by the opposite method, promising the reader that he is dealing in pure fact. The advantage of fact over realistic fiction has been insightfully stated by Nathalie Sarraute in *The Age of Suspicion*:

The "true fact" has indeed an indubitable advantage over the invented tale. To begin with, that of being true. This is the source of its strength of conviction and forcefulness, of its noble indifference to ridicule and bad taste, also of a certain quiet daring, a certain off-handedness, that allows it to break through the confining limitations in which a regard for likelihood imprisons the boldest of novelists, and to extend far afield the frontiers of reality. It allows us to attain to unknown regions into which no writer would have dared venture, and brings us, with one leap, to the edge of the "abyss." [20]

The realistic novelist must convince the reader of plausible motivation, larger forces, or at least an acceptable level of coincidence. He says to the reader, *All this did not really happen, but it could have.* Credibility has different meanings and obligations for the fabulist and new journalist, however. The fabulist need only convince on the basis of the internal cohesion of his purely imaginary works. He says, *All this could never happen, so do not blame me if it does not seem real.* The new journalist, on the other hand, need only convince on the basis of verifiable sources and his personal integrity: *All this actually did happen, so do not blame me if it does not seem real.*

The fiction writer and new journalist have both leapt over the contemporary breakdown of the classic contractual agreement between author and reader based on notions of plausibility and "suspension of disbelief." Moreover, they have both, by this same leap, solved the problem of a lack of a stable body of manners and morals. By giving up all claims to the actual world, the fabulator frees himself from its vagaries and can deal instead in the more universal elements of idea and pattern. Likewise, by claiming the actual world as the content of his works, the new journalist justifies writing directly about the phenomena of contemporary life. Rather than trying to use transient and diverse phenomena as self-evident signals of meaning, he can deal with them directly, attempting to decipher their literal and larger significance. Their ephemerality and strangeness are themselves often major subjects of his works.

In this way the fiction writer and the new journalist are free to deal with the most stressful concerns of contemporary America. While the first insists on fantasy, the second claims fact. But both assert the necessity of an imaginative, pattern-making consciousness. Faced with breakdown in the actual world, the writer of fabulist fiction frees himself as far as possible from all relationship with it, turning inward to create a world with a meaningful design. Thus Barth creates his own cosmos in *Giles Goat-Boy*, and Pynchon describes a World War II that never happened in *Gravity's Rainbow*. Confronted with the same problem, the new journalist ties himself inexorably to the actual world but turns his imagination outward to create a meaningful design from his experience of it. Thus Mailer constructs a mock-heroic epic from his experience of a protest march in *The Armies of the Night*, and Wolfe shapes Ken Kesey's drug-related adventures into a tragic quest in *The Electric Kool-Aid Acid Test*. Both the fiction writer and the new journalist have abandoned the relatively luxurious concerns and methods of the realistic novelist in a stable society, instead focusing on the more basic powers of fiction—the ordering of a meaningful world, and the defining of a relationship with it.

The alteration in American experience during the 1960's is now widely acknowledged as the problem to which writers of fabulist fiction and new journalism have responded. Mas'ud Zavarzadeh in *The Mythopoeic Reality* and John Hollowell in *Fact and Fiction* discuss this aspect of new journalistic writing in some detail.[21] Literary observers have generally been much slower to perceive the close relationship between the experimental techniques of these two forms. As indicated earlier, Wolfe himself claims that new journalism is simply a fulfillment of the techniques and aims of realism (see especially his "Introduction" to *The New Journalism*). But as D. H. Lawrence said of the significance of earlier American writers, we should "never trust the artist. Trust the tale." Wolfe's claim is clearly belied by the fable-like texture and form of his own works. A number of observers have noted this quality. Robert J. Van Dellen, for instance, dismisses Wolfe's claim of realism as a disguise for a form that is actually "artificially mythic" and "its own kind of fable."[22] Wilfrid Sheed has said that Wolfe's claims to be a realist in his reportage are "like El Greco boasting about his photographic accuracy," and has asserted that the effect of Wolfe's *Radical Chic* is "gorgeously unreal."[23] Dwight Macdonald, the most notorious debunker of the new journalism, has viewed the same quality less positively, complaining that Wolfe's subjects may be real, but they somehow emerge as "freely invented" in his "parajournalistic" works.[24] The discrepancy between Wolfe's claims that new journalism is the ultimate realism and the actual nature of his own work may be understood if we view his assertions as a calculated response to literary and journalistic attacks on the validity of his work. Certainly, it will not serve as an accurate description of even his own new journalism. (For a more extensive consideration of Wolfe's claims, see Chapter 5.)

Despite the opposite nature of their author-reader contracts, new journalists share with contemporary fiction writers an emphasis upon the perceiving consciousness as a transforming power, and a desire to avoid the distortion caused by an attempt to disguise that power. As a result, the two forms have many technical and thematic similarities. Both, for instance, often organize their materials into narratives "framed" by forewords, afterwords, or other devices. Both use a self-conscious and highly obtrusive narrator, alter the usual conventions of punctuation or

graphic composition, and are either episodic or obviously contrived (instead of conventionally patterned to and from a climax). Both use allegorical and mythic patterns drawn from
classical and popular-culture sources, have heavily mannered
styles, and adopt a stance of parody or satire. They are also
characterized by a concern with large philosophical and social
issues.[25] In subsequent chapters we will see how these elements
figure in new journalistic works. Here it would be revealing
merely to note how those traits relating to the author's assertion
of his controlling presence are found in both contemporary
fabulist fiction and new journalism, in direct contrast to their
usual absence or suppression in realistic fiction.

In contemporary fiction and new journalism, forewords or
afterwords often explain the origins of the work and the circumstances under which it was created. This is true of Vonnegut's *Mother Night* as well as of Thompson's *Fear and Loathing:
On the Campaign Trail '72*, of Nabokov's *Pale Fire* as well as of
Capote's *In Cold Blood*. The fiction writer provides such appa-
ratus as clear fakery in order to draw attention to the traditional
status of fiction as a masquerade of reality. The effect is to
obviously "frame" the work, and thus to set it off from reality.
The new journalist, on the other hand, frames his work in order
to convince the reader that the *opposite* is the case—that it is a
"true account" based on actual observation and years of research. By discussing his original involvement in the events, his
sources' extremely vivid memories, or his characters' reactions to
their first reading of his manuscript, the new journalist is able to
strengthen his reader's perception of the work's link to actuality.

Yet the effect of the new journalist's foreword or afterword is
really rather ambiguous. However much it may serve as evidence
of fact, its position *outside* the work also reinforces the reader's
perception of the fictional form, and thus the *structuring* of an
experience by the author, that the work embodies. The new
journalist's "framing" of his work emphasizes the factual nature
of the content (strengthening his journalistic contract), while in a
seeming paradox drawing attention to the fictional shape of the
form (acknowledging the role of his organizing consciousness).

Contemporary experimental fiction and new journalistic
works share many more similarities in the central role of the

author as transforming agent, similarities that contrast sharply to the conventions of realistic fiction. In both forms the author is often visibly present as either a narrator or a character or both. In the fabulist novel *Gravity's Rainbow*, for instance, Thomas Pynchon follows a practice Wolfe had established in *The Electric Kool-Aid Acid Test*, actually badgering his characters from a position which is difficult to locate as quite within or without the fiction. (Wolfe calls this the "Hectoring Narrator.") The self-conscious narrator who enjoys discussing his characters with the reader, intruding upon the narrative, and in some cases chatting about his problems in simply telling the story, is an important aspect of contemporary fiction—so important that works which are organized on the principle of being about themselves form a subgenre called metafiction. (The method has clear roots in such eighteenth-century works as *Tristram Shandy*.) These methods are also apparent in new journalistic works. For instance, Mailer openly discusses his journalistic and authorial strategies and characters in *The Armies of the Night*; he constructs *Of a Fire on the Moon* as a book about trying to write a book about the moon flight. Likewise, Thompson turns his problems of composition into one of the central mock-dramas of *Campaign Trail*.

These narrative devices function like the "framing" forewords and afterwords in reminding the reader that the work has a created form and perspective. It is something "made," a fiction with a necessarily ambiguous relation to the actual world outside the author's transforming experience and reflection. In this way the author reminds readers of the necessarily central position of his shaping consciousness, whether he be inventor or reporter. Even when an author does not use any of the above narrative devices (Robert Coover and Capote rarely do) he tends to write in a highly distinctive, even mannered style which inevitably calls attention to his presence as a transforming agent. But while critics of contemporary fiction often praise this self-conscious emphasis upon artifice for its acknowledgment of the true function and status of the fiction-making process in the world, critics of new journalism have more often failed to notice it, or have attacked it as an egotistic failure to concentrate on the job of reporting.

In its "Newswatch" column, for instance, *Newsweek* traced

the self-conscious and seemingly self-absorbed "detours" of a
Hunter Thompson article on Jimmy Carter before responding to
the promise of some discussion of the candidate's positions on
the issues by exclaiming, "At last we are getting down to it!" [26]
And literary critic Wayne Booth has complained that "the thesis
of *Loathing* is that Hunter Thompson is interesting." [27] Actually, while self-indulgence is clearly a danger here, such reminders
of the new journalist's shaping presence (and at times concentration upon it) are an essential aspect of his strategy for presenting
his subjects as they are experienced and engaged by a human
consciousness.

These devices emphasizing the work as a product of external
world and internal mind enable the authors of contemporary
fiction and new journalism to draw attention to the all-important
role of imagination in dealing with either the imaginary or the
factual. For while the fiction writer and the new journalist have
established exactly opposed contracts with their readers, they
both intend to obtain a basis for their highly imaginative
approaches to the problematic nature of contemporary reality, a
basis stronger than the realist has enjoyed. This is the central
assumption of the experimental strategies by which both the
fiction writer and the new journalist deal with contemporary
American reality: the power of an individual consciousness to
perceive pattern in experience.

While realistic fiction is a product of the author's creative
imagination, it has, as a rule, played down the role of this
transforming power in order to accentuate the illusion of reality
for its fabrications. The emphasis is on verisimilitude or, more
exactly, its semblance. The contemporary fiction writer and the
new journalist have cut themselves loose from these problems by
forging new contracts with the reader, thus freeing themselves to
acknowledge and exploit the formative and metaphoric powers
of their imaginations. The fabulist writer says, *I have abandoned
the real, so I have only my imaginative creations to give you*. The
new journalist says, *I have tied myself completely to the actual,
but I can give it to you only as I have humanly, and thus
imaginatively, experienced and recollected it*. The same emphasis
on the creative power of imagination that led Barth to admit that
what he "really wants to do is re-invent the world" [28] led Mailer

to give his history the form of a novel. (The experiments of Barth, Mailer, and others have been followed by works that seem to have more confusing author-reader contracts: John Fowles's *French Lieutenant's Woman*, E. L. Doctorow's *Ragtime*, Robert Coover's *Public Burning*. While these works represent an interesting third route of experimentation, their author-reader contracts are essentially the same as those of the fabulist writers, since they allow themselves the most outrageous divergence from fact, however closely they may often adhere to it. When new journalists use fantasy or invention—in Thompson's *Campaign Trail*, for example—they usually signal the reader in some way.[29])

These two major innovations of contemporary "fabulist" fiction and new journalism, the separate contracts and the similar emphasis upon imagination, have enabled them to overcome the contemporary crisis in realistic fiction in order to better deal with a new experience of reality. Working from opposite agreements with the reader concerning the nature of their relationships to reality, the two forms nevertheless both work toward fabulist forms and concerns. Finding a fragmented reality, they avoid representation and seek construction.

There are, of course, precedents to contemporary new journalism and nonfiction novels, and they have been listed and discussed many times. Anthony Burgess has said that "Mailer is using a very much earlier technique than anything the 20th Century has discovered—the technique of Daniel Defoe, of either presenting reality in the form of a novel or presenting the materials of a novel in the form of reality." [30] This statement is both correct and potentially misleading. There is no "form of reality"; rather, there are forms which we associate with reality as a result of long-standing convention. The new journalist presents fact in fictional form, but it is fiction only in the more sophisticated and original sense of the word that has led Northrop Frye to apply it to any "work of art in prose." [31]

Robert Scholes, one of our most lucid theoreticians of narrative, has provided a suggestive discussion of the artificially dichotomized relationship between fact and fiction by going back to their similar roots: "Fact comes from *facere*—to make or do. Fiction comes from *fingere*—to make or shape." [32] This return to the two words' etymological roots suggests the difference between reporting and fictionalizing as described by Hemingway, who of course made major contributions to both:

If it was reporting they would not remember it. When you describe something that has happened that day the timeliness makes people see it in their own imaginations. A month later that element of time is gone and your account would be flat and they would not see it in their minds nor remember it. But if you make it up instead of describe it you can make it round and whole and solid and give it life. You create it, for good or bad. It is made; not described. It is just as true as the extent of your ability to make it and knowledge you put into it. [33]

Frye, Scholes, and Hemingway all indicate that there is no strict difference between "fact" and "fiction" as found in their popular connotations of "truth" and "falsehood." Rather, they involve two distinct activities that can be left separate or merged. The new journalist has chosen to use fiction as a way of knowing and communicating fact. He has made this choice because fiction is the type of writing that provides the most effective means of dramatizing the complexities and ambiguities of experience—the dynamic and fluid wholeness of an event as it is felt and ordered ("made") by a human consciousness.

There are dangers in this process. The writer, finding a tension between the requirements of a true account of his subject and those of a strong narrative, may sacrifice truth for effect by overly dramatizing. When this occurs, new journalism becomes simply a version of the "yellow journalism" against which today's conventional journalism was partly a response. Some new journalists have occasionally sacrificed accuracy of individual facts for atmosphere and effect. But this breaking of the journalistic contract invalidates the works involved, not the genre as a whole (in fact, new journalistic works are typically researched in great detail). Finally, the use of such fictional techniques as composite characters and compressed narratives, while actually having a long tradition in journalism, certainly violates the journalistic contract. If they are revealed to the reader, they turn the work into realistic fiction with strong elements of reportage. If not revealed (as was the case with Gail Sheehy's *New York* articles on prostitution) they are clearly unfair distortions of the subject. One of the crucial problems for a new journalist is to find the fictional methods by which he can shape his narrative without destroying its journalistic status. His apparent success or failure must be considered basic to the criteria by which we judge his work.

In the 1960's an alteration in American experience led writers of both fiction and journalism to make artistic forays into each other's territory. New journalism is new because it made two necessarily radical alterations in the previous forms. First, it overcame the weaknesses of the traditional fictional contract, in which the author promised plausibility, by replacing it with a journalistic one promising factuality; second, it overcame the limitations of conventional journalism and realistic fiction by exploiting fully and frankly the power of shaping consciousness found in fabulist fiction. The result was a new form both wholly fictional and wholly journalistic through which the individual human consciousness could directly make or organize the seemingly chaotic world into a work embodying a meaningful engagement of the two.

New journalism is new for the same basic reasons that contemporary fiction is new. Both were forced by an implausible reality into radical breaks with the traditional author-reader contract. Both sought new powers for the imagination by drawing on the technical advances of the moderns as well as turning all the way back to the eighteenth century and earlier for forgotten devices and conventions they could manipulate into new freedoms and possibilities. But the demanding new duties of fiction to somehow shape a meaningful world and define a vital relationship with it also led inexorably to a third similarity between the two forms: their similar function as "artificial myths" or fables.

In the next chapter I will outline a theory providing a critical framework with which to approach the genre—without falling into simplistic fact-fiction debate, and without imposing a narrow conception on it. I will then turn to the four authors who have acquired the most stature in the new journalism and who have been most innovative in developing individual approaches to the form. These authors vary widely in approach—from Mailer's often prophetic and epic tone to Thompson's fierce caricatures, from Wolfe's stylistic and analytic distance from the events he reports to Herr's intense exploration of his participation in them—but each combines a journalistic contract with a frank acknowledgment and exploration of the crucially central role of a transforming consciousness. They have been chosen over such authors as Capote and Talese because the latter have been less artistically innovative, more traditional and impersonal in their use of fictional resources to portray fact. Capote's *In Cold Blood*, for instance, shares many of the concerns and methods discussed in this chapter and is of obvious importance in the development and recognition of new journalism; still, it is a transitional work which is close to conventional journalism in the illusion of objectivity Capote seeks through an impersonal, omniscient point of view, and close to realistic fiction in the limitations of its rather conservative techniques. In contrast, and like the fabulators, the four new journalists I will consider have assertively broadened the realm of fictive possibilities in their attempts to find pattern and meaning in a postmodern reality defying traditional approaches.

2

The Nature and Modes of the New Journalism: A Theory

The basic premise of this study is that new journalism is a genre of fiction, even as it is resolutely factual if it fulfills its obligations to its reader. The apparent confusion in the fact-fiction terminology (with *The Executioner's Song* and *The Right Stuff* nominated in the fiction and the nonfiction categories, respectively, for the 1979 American Book Awards) that has kept most discussion of the form at the level of debate over preconceptions, rather than study of the actual achievements of the works, is only apparently a paradox. For the terms suggest a polarity, by subject, of "types" of writing that actually possess separate forms and purposes. The major division in types of writing, as Frye has pointed out, is between the literary and the descriptive or assertive. If we accept Frye's definition of fiction as literary prose, then our division is properly between the fictional and the assertive. This reformulation of the issues eliminates the unfortunate *illusory* separation of fictional and factual writing—illusory because it seems to separate aesthetic form and purpose from a certain subject matter: fact. In this chapter I will set forth a theoretical framework for discussing these works as a major genre of contemporary fiction.

There have been two major attempts to explain the nature of the new journalistic form. The first is Tom Wolfe's theory (expanded somewhat by Hollowell in *Fact and Fiction*) that new journalism involves the application of specific devices of realistic fiction to materials gathered by exhaustive reportage. But while this definition suggests the crucial merging of fictional form and purpose with factual subject matter, even a cursory look at such works as Mailer's *Of a Fire on the Moon*, Thompson's *Fear and Loathing: On the Campaign Trail '72*, or Herr's *Dispatches* shows how little of a new journalistic work can involve Wolfe's devices of scene-by-scene construction, recording of dialogue, providing of status details, and narration through a point of view other than the author's. Wolfe himself has admitted in other places that he could only make *The Electric Kool-Aid Acid Test* and *The Right Stuff* work by abandoning strict adherence to these techniques in favor of summary narration and exposition.[1] In addition, Wolfe and Hollowell, by suggesting that new journalism is consistently realistic, narrowly define the genre in terms of a single mode, when actually the major works reveal a much more diverse and innovative range of experimentation. Finally, in a penetrating review-essay Barbara Foley has pointed out that there are serious logical difficulties in defining a genre by "quantification," for it immediately places works having only some of these devices in an ambiguous area.[2]

A very different theory has been proposed by Mas'ud Zavarzadeh in *The Mythopoeic Reality*. Using the term "nonfiction novel," which he rather arbitrarily distinguishes from new journalism,[3] Zavarzadeh argues that the fact-fiction polarity that he accepts as valid for other works has been merged by this new genre. Factual and fictional writing, he says, are "monoreferential" types that refer ultimately in one direction: the fictional is "in-referential," gaining credibility solely by "internal consistency"; the factual is "out-referential," acquiring credibility by its correlation with "the external world." The nonfiction novel is a new type of writing, unique because it is "bireferential," simultaneously pointing to the external world and to its own text. Because of its unique status, he feels that discussion of the form requires a new set of critical assumptions and terms: plot must be replaced with "acteme" and characters with "people" (subdivided by relation to the acteme into "actant" and "actee"). And, just as Wolfe and Hollowell would restrict new journalism to realistic techniques, Zavarzadeh asserts that the nonfiction novelists are uniformly absurdists in their intention, as they feel that they "can only neutrally transcribe the texture of the fictional reality whose contradictory nature and mythic dimensions resist the totalizing imagination."[4]

A satisfactory theory of the new journalism must be based more closely on observation of what actually occurs in the texts,

rather than imposing Wolfe's realism or Zavarzadeh's absurd-
ism. New journalistic works share a factual subject matter and an
aesthetic form and purpose. This aesthetic, or fictional, aspect of
a text in any literary genre is not a matter of certain techniques or
of a specific philosophical view; rather, it is the construction of
the text, whatever its subject, as a work of artistic design and
intention so that it finally, or ultimately, refers to itself. As E. M.
Forster said, "Art stands still, History moves on." All writing, to
use Zavarzadeh's term, is "bireferential," referring both outside
the text to a subject and inside to other elements within the text.
The distinction between literary and assertive writing, as Frye
has convincingly argued, is determined by the final direction of
the reference:

> Whenever we read anything, we find our attention moving in two
> directions at once. One direction is outward or centrifugal, in which we
> keep going outside our reading, from the individual words to the things
> they mean, or, in practice, to our memory of the conventional associa-
> tion between them. The other direction is inward or centripetal, in
> which we try to develop from the words a sense of the larger verbal
> pattern they make.   . . . .
>
> But verbal structures may be classified according to whether the *final*
> direction of meaning is outward or inward. In descriptive or assertive
> writing the final direction is outward. Here the verbal structure is
> intended to represent things external to it, and it is valued in terms of the
> accuracy with which it does represent them. Correspondence between
> phenomenon and verbal sign is truth; lack of it is falsehood; failure to
> connect is tautology, a purely verbal structure that cannot come out of
> itself.
>
> In all literary verbal structures the final direction of meaning is
> inward.[5]

There is a crucial difference between Zavarzadeh's distinction
between fictional and factual writing as two distinct "mono-
referential" forms and Frye's concept of all writing as bireferential but separated into literary or descriptive according to
"final," or ultimate, direction.

By "final" direction of reference Frye is speaking, in my understanding, of the effect achieved by the selection and the arrange-
ment of the textual elements. If the elements of a text are selected
and arranged with regard to their relation to the external world,

that text is finally assertive. If they are selected and arranged with regard to their relation to each other, a world is created by their relations in the text, making that text finally literary. In the former case, the finally assertive text may subsume techniques or effects which are in themselves literary, resulting in a finally assertive text with literary texture. Or, in the latter case, the finally literary text may subsume elements which are in themselves assertive, providing a finally literary text with considerable assertive interest. Works such as the Declaration of Independence, Boswell's *Life of Johnson*, and the Bible may seem to call Frye's distinction into question. The Declaration of Independence was clearly written with an important, immediate assertive purpose. Likewise, the *Life of Samuel Johnson* offers information about its subject, and the Bible includes precepts. All three of these works, however, subsume their assertive aspects within a form giving them an interest and value beyond their direct relation to the external world to which their elements correspond. Each has been so constructed that the elements of the text create relations establishing an experience in the text. Thus these works have a literary value, a continuing experience and import available to readers whether or not their immediate subjects or purposes are of interest.

The new journalism is, in my view, most properly understood as a genre of literature. Like realistic fiction or romantic fiction or fabulist fiction, it has an aesthetic form and purpose making its "final direction" inward. Following Frye's definition (quoted in the preceding chapter) that fiction is "a work of art in prose," [6] we may then without logical difficulty call new journalism fiction. A work of conventional journalism, in contrast, clearly falls within the category of "descriptive or assertive writing" in which the final direction is outward. This is also true of most works of history and sociology. We think of the works of Capote, Mailer, Wolfe, Herr, Thompson, and other new journalists as members of a single genre, despite their being spread throughout the Library of Congress in different categories according to subject, because we recognize, if only intuitively, the primacy of their shared aesthetic form and purpose. In order to penetrate the current confusion with which these works are viewed, we must

make a similar recognition on an explicitly analytic and theoretical level, realizing that literary critics can no longer hold the
popular subject-centered notion of fictional and factual writing
as invention and recording, respectively. Instead, we must speak
of different kinds of writing either in terms of their relation to
subject, or in terms of their final direction of meaning, and not try
to speak in the one way by reference to the other.

The primary importance of an aesthetic form which ultimately
determines the selection and presentation of facts is what I think
Mailer has been suggesting by subtitling Book I of *The Armies of
the Night* "History As a Novel" and *The Executioner's Song* "A
True Life Novel," as well as by asserting in the preface to *Some
Honorable Men* that "the world (not the techniques but the
world) of fiction can be brought to the facts of journalism." [7] In a
work of new journalism the author is most interested in the effect
and idea he can communicate by form. However exhaustive or
important his reporting or analysis may be, his ultimate aim and
achievement is an artistic one.

In the works of Mailer, Wolfe, Thompson and Herr, we will
see that the various journalistic elements of the text are selected,
arranged, and stylistically transformed so that they create an
aesthetic experience embodying the author's personal experience
and interpretation of the subject. Each author transforms his
journalistic subject into a living text so that the reader does
not merely read about events, but participates in the author's
personal experience and interpretation of them. A reader goes to
Mailer's political journalism, for instance, not primarily for journalistic information but for the experience and lessons to be
acquired from participating in his intensely meditative journey
through our times. Likewise, a reader goes to Thompson's "fear
and loathing" to enjoy the power of the manic comic vision with
which he counters the horrors we otherwise receive only passively in the news. In other words, the new journalists give us what
literary artists have always given us—only they do so in direct
confrontation with the news that has become our major shared
experience in a media age. Their works are aesthetic experiences
embodying the result of this confrontation between external
events and personal mind—a microcosmic selection, shaping,

and interpretation of events of the macrocosm into a text, a construct representing not events, but an individual consciousness's experience of them.

The way to simplify the problems in discussing this genre in order to penetrate the apparent paradoxes of the fact-fiction polarity is to reformulate the terms of our discussion. If we place genres of writing on two separate spectra, we can avoid false polarities. All genres of literary prose, or fiction by Frye's definition, belong on one spectrum; writing that is primarily "assertive" or outward-pointing should be considered as ranging on a separate spectrum. Once we see the genres of ultimately inward-pointing writing on a plane of their own, we can distinguish between these genres of fiction by looking at how the works also point outward. Here we find that, having rid ourselves of confusion as to why the forms are related, we may easily see why they are distinct. Each points outward to a different subject. Realism points to an external world that appears to be *like* the actual world recognized as credible by most readers. In truth, this world is abstracted by the author from his observations of actual people and events, and then concretized as characters and incidents either very close to or quite dissimilar from actual ones, but in any case never violating basic principles of plausibility or, for the most part, altering actual details of milieu. Silas Lapham and Jake Barnes, for instance, may or may not be based on actual persons, but they succeed as realistic characters because they refer us to recognizable types moving through a particular milieu of the actual world. We may know that world either from experience or from reading, but in either case we know it from outside the texts of *The Rise of Silas Lapham* and *The Sun Also Rises*. Romance points to a world external to the text in which our observations of the actual world are abstracted, and then *idealized*, before being concretized as components of a finer and more perfectly shaped world than we can readily accept as actual. Fabulation points to a world external to the text in which observations of the actual are abstracted and radically altered, perhaps severely restricted or expanded or turned upside down, before being concretized as components of a world we know to exist only in the minds of the author and reader. (Note that even the most fantastic or cerebral fabulation of Borges or Barth is not self-contained, but relies on pointing the reader outside the text, even if to drastically altered versions of the actual world.)

New journalism is the genre of fiction in which the text, while (like other genres of fiction) pointing finally or ultimately inward, points outward toward the actual world without ever deviating from observations of that world except in forms—such as authorial speculation or fantasy—which are immediately obvious as such to the reader. To be more precise, the world pointed to is a journalistic one; it adheres to "primary sources" of a first-hand nature, either the author's observations or his gathering of others' observations of events occurring around the time of authorship. This strictly journalistic subject distinguishes a work of new journalism from a historical novel, which may at its closest to new journalism point to a world *based on* an actual historical one but which, because of remoteness in time and the secondary, limited nature of sources, must almost always include considerable invention (detail, dialogue, usually entire scenes) if the text is to have sufficient texture to work as an experiential object. For similar reasons, Mailer's *Marilyn* is not a work of new journalism, for its nearly exclusive dependence on secondary sources (other biographies) and speculation causes it to point to a world considerably more removed from the actual. The differences that I am asserting between the genres of the realistic novel, romance, fabulation, historical novel, and new journalism, as well as other genres one might choose to add, are then determined by the direction outside the text to which the text points (while ultimately always pointing within to the fictional world the text creates through its aesthetic form). This identification of the relation of text to external world as the crux of any distinction between genres of fiction brings us back to the concept of author-reader contract developed in the preceding chapter: an assertion by the author and acceptance by the reader of the particular relation of the text to an external world, the direction in which it points. This contract or agreement between author and reader has a crucial effect on *how* a text is experienced. While the final, overall effect of a fictional text is by definition the result of how the components of the text refer to each other in comprising an aesthetic form, that final effect is influenced by what direction the reader believes it is pointing out toward.

The Armies of the Night, if read by a person somehow ignorant or disbelieving of its journalistic contract (its claim to adherence to actual observation), would be a somewhat—probably considerably—altered aesthetic experience. Indeed, if audiences read them as realistic novels rather than as new journalism, many such works would seem so incredible that they would collapse as aesthetic experiences, rejected by the reader as violations of the rules of plausibility and common sense laid down by the contract of realistic fiction. Conversely, a work of fabulation, if somehow accepted by the reader as a work of journalism, would become a distinctly different aesthetic experience. (The transformation of H. G. Wells's science-fiction novel *War of the Worlds* into a 1930's too-effective imitation of a journalistic radio broadcast caused many listeners to mistake the invented fable for reported fact, and to respond by fleeing their homes.) Thus we see that, in clear refutation of a strictly formalist approach, an important aspect of the aesthetic effect of any work of literature is determined by the relation, promised by the author and agreed to by the reader, of text to external world.

A contract, of course, has no legitimacy or effect unless it is accepted and adhered to by both parties. A new journalist's integrity, efforts, and talents as a journalist, as well as his ability to convey these traits, are therefore an important and legitimate aspect of a critic's evaluation of a work in this genre. Since the validity and credibility of the journalistic author-reader contract are intrinsic to the aesthetic effect of such a work, these aspects of the text are equally proper subjects of study as style and manipulation of point of view. (Such a determination of journalistic validity in a work of new journalism can now be seen as a proper object of critical evaluation, no different from considering the maintenance of a consistent tone in the most assertively incredible of fabulations, for in that way a fabulist maintains his commitment to create an autonomous but coherent world.)

An author can make a convincing journalistic contract in a number of ways. The first, simplest, and very effective method is simply to say so: to have the book labeled as nonfiction. (Hence, as we have seen, the critical confusion.) The author can strengthen this claim by explaining in framing devices (forewords, afterwords, epilogues, etc.) that the book adheres completely to his own or others' observations. He can develop this into a detailed description of materials available to him, or he can place various documents and externally verifiable data within the text. Finally, he can in various ways, such as through unusual self-revelations, convince the reader of his honesty and trustworthiness. If an author somehow causes the reader to have serious doubts about the validity of the journalistic contract, the aesthetic effect is altered or lessened, and this should properly affect critical evaluation. I would argue, for instance, that this is an important aspect in evaluating Mailer's *Executioner's Song* in comparison to Capote's *In Cold Blood*. Mailer makes more reasonable claims of knowledge and less manipulative use of point of view. Even the relatively subtle difference of researched fact presented as observed fact creates a different reading experience. Certainly the modern understanding of Defoe's *Journal of the Plague Year* as a carefully researched and considerably accurate deception alters our experience of the text from that of Defoe's contemporary readers, who read it as firsthand factual report.

Once he has explored the relation of the new journalistic work to its subject, a critic may move to his primary or final task in approaching any work of fiction—the exploration of the method and effect of the aesthetic form. While Wolfe's approach would straitjacket the form into four specific devices which he identifies with realistic fiction, we can freely explore the diverse methods of a form that is fiction by its experiential, aesthetic nature. We may use the same concepts of criticism applied to other works of fiction, as long as we heed the special obligations and limits set up by the specific author-reader contract promising a journalistic relation of text to external world. Thus, in clear contradiction to Zavarzadeh's assertions, traditional concepts of plot and character are perfectly applicable to critical approaches to these works. Indeed, we may confidently draw upon virtually the entire range of technical terms associated with the criticism of fiction, for examination of new journalistic texts reveals the presence of both the most basic and the most sophisticated devices of fiction developed from the eighteenth century through modernism to the present era, from characterization to stream-of-consciousness, from symbolism to manipulation of an unreliable narrator, from suspense to fragmented narrative.

Zavarzadeh asserts that E. M. Forster's concept of "flat" and "round" characterization, the notion of plot, and the effect of suspense can have no relevance to a work that is about actual people and events.[8] To support his assertion about characterization, he opposes William Gass's observation that characters are "made by words, out of words" to Oscar Lewis's statement that in the nonfiction novel they "are not constructed types but are real people."[9] This opposition ignores the fact that any individual in a work of writing—whether existing *outside* the text as a figment of fantasy, or as an actual person—exists *within* the text as a verbal construct. Gass's assertion holds for the work of new journalism. Any attempt by an author to put a living person on a page can result, because of the nature of language (indeed, of perception), only in a verbal construct—a character—that is comprised of the author's impressions of the living person and his inevitably interpretive selection and ordering of those impressions, and, finally, his mediation of that interpretation through language. Even the most objectively motivated and denotatively stylistic authors must do this. All one must do to realize the truth, in this aesthetic sense, of the inevitably fictional nature of a character in a literary text is to try to imagine transferring the relatively complex, "round" Hubert Humphrey of Mailer's *St. George and the Godfather* to Thompson's *Fear and Loathing: On the Campaign Trail '72*, and inserting the two-dimensional, parodic Humphrey of that latter work in Mailer's book. One would immediately encounter the same difficulty René Wellek suggests, in quoting Desmond McCarthy on invented characters in traditional novels: "Imagine, McCarthy says, 'a character moved from one imaginary world to another. If Pecksniff were transplanted into *The Golden Bowl* he would become extinct. . . . The unforgivable artistic fault in a novelist is failure to maintain consistency of tone.' "[10]

The fact that the reader encounters either Mailer's or Thompson's text with a previous conception of Humphrey does not alter the validity of this interpretation, any more than does a reader's knowledge of Napoleon before encountering the Napoleon in *War and Peace*. For that matter, a reader may know Freud in history and Sherlock Holmes in fiction before encountering Nicholas Meyer's characters in *The Seven Per-Cent Solution*. (Though, because the reader knows Holmes previously from fictional texts, Meyer knows that Holmes must be made convincing for the reader not only by accuracy to "facts" *about* him drawn from the Conan Doyle stories, but also by imitation of the stylistic texture, the fictional "world," of Doyle's works.) Indeed, the Hubert Humphrey that the reader knows outside his experience of a text is an interpretively selected and ordered construct of impressions, as is the author's, whether arrived at through first-hand knowledge or (more typically) already interpreted as received from the mass media. The existence of a version of the character independent from the author's creation raises special opportunities and problems for the author. He may find it easier to make the character credible, in the superficial sense of convincing the reader that a Humphrey exists; but he may find it more difficult in the more crucial sense of convincing the reader that *his* Humphrey is legitimate, in relation to the actual Humphrey of the world outside the text. Again, this is an aspect of the relation of text to external world—to be compared to, yet seen as distinct from, the problem of a realistic novelist in making an invented character seem *lifelike*. It does not negate the observation that Mailer's or Thompson's Humphrey is finally a separate construct of each author's fictional world. Each points in factual relation to the Humphrey of the actual world, but belongs ultimately to that fictional world of the text.

We may similarly deny Zavarzadeh's claim that the nonfiction novel has no "plot" in the traditional sense because the author "cannot change or modify it in order to convey a private vision through it." [11] The journalistic contract should, of course, prevent an author in this genre from altering factual elements, and will probably even forbid the omission of many details. Any nonfiction novel concerning the 1972 conventions will probably include, as part of the plot, the nominations of Nixon and McGovern. Certainly, unless clear authorial fantasy is being temporarily indulged in (as when in *Campaign Trail* Thompson fantasizes releasing bats in the hall at the moment of Humphrey's nomination), such a work could not change a factual element. Nevertheless, the author's freedom to select and arrange a sequence of events remains considerable, so that Mailer's "plot" in *St. George and the Godfather* and Thompson's in the parts of *Campaign Trail* dealing with the conventions are considerably different.

The applicability of standard terms of literary criticism is further evident when one examines Zavarzadeh's assertion that the "grouping of actemes in the nonfiction novel is also without that dominant characteristic of the fictive plot traditionally identified as 'suspense'—the conventional anticipation and expectation of the reader about the development of situations in the narrative." [12] Anyone who has viewed Alfred Hitchcock's *Psycho* more than once will recognize that suspense hinges not on ignorance of the imminent course of events, but on the skillful construction of the sequence. A first-time or second-time reader of *In Cold Blood* will likely, and chillingly, report the same. But even the particular kind of suspense created by "mystery," which appears to be what Zavarzadeh means, may be created in a nonfiction novel by the author's focusing the narrative development on a lesser-known element or on a deeper question than "what happens next." In *In Cold Blood*, for instance, Capote creates considerable suspense of this sort by holding off the account of the murders until long after the discovery of the victims in the narrative. And in Book II of *The Executioner's Song* Mailer creates a mounting mystery concerning how the events of Book I finally came into the hands of the author. (He takes the reader to the solution without actually naming it.) Indeed, in Part II of *Of a Fire on the Moon* Mailer creates suspense by making his attempt to construct a meaningful account of the moon flight the dramatic focus of the narrative. Taking this metafictional tactic yet further, in *Campaign Trail* Thompson creates a parodic melodrama out of his frantic attempts, while waging a battle with raging digression and paranoid hallucination, to force his pressured consciousness to construct a coherent report in the face of monthly deadlines. Any one of these examples of the creation of suspense in a nonfiction novel should further serve to show how much "plot" freedom an author actually has in the genre. Indeed, these examples should indicate how the challenge of a particular journalistic subject can stimulate narrative experimentation.

The preceding discussion has, I hope, established that the new journalism is properly understood as a genre of fiction. Apparent critical dilemmas are solved by recognizing that, like any writing, new journalism points to an external subject; but, like traditional novels, romances, fabulations, and historical novels, it is fiction because it finally points to its own form. Our standard critical terms for discussion of fiction therefore remain valid, demanding only the same degree of qualification and separate criteria of evaluation required when one moves from consideration of a realistic novel to a romance or fabulation. Finally, the precise mode of a new journalistic work may be realistic, surrealistic, naturalistic, parodic, ironic, romantic, or whatever. When we turn from the boundaries of a text described by generic definition to the possibilities described by mode, an author's version of the actual world as manifest through language and form in the text may create a pattern, without violating facts, fitting any of the terms above. With a critical framework that enables us to understand new journalism as a form of fiction with a subject of journalistic fact, we will be better able to explore the rich, individual approaches to fact of separate texts. Indeed, one of the most exciting because so clearly problematic aspects of new journalism thus becomes apparent—the relation of language and form, of text, of knowledge, of meaningful construction to the external world, however empirically determined and exhaustively observed. It is a central issue of literature on which works of new journalism perhaps most sharply focus.

In the following chapters I study individual works with the aim of showing how artists have been able to find, in the genre of new journalism, rich and diverse literary (fictional, by Frye's definition) possibilities while adhering to a journalistic author-reader contract. In developing fictional freedom to create a unique aesthetic experience, these authors have consistently approached the journalistic contract through the self-reflexive strategies associated with fabulation. External facts may be presented in various modes, because the text is clearly a construct of an individual consciousness; i.e., the ultimate ontological status of the work is clearly not as an objective representation of the actual world, but as the personal construct of a shaping, selecting, interpretive mind. Thus two nonfiction novels on one subject create two worlds, even as they point to a factual one. Through the self-conscious strategy recognized as central to the fabulator, the new journalist creates his fables of fact.

3

Journalism as Metafiction: Norman Mailer's Strategy for Mimesis and Interpretation in a Postmodern World

Well, Aquarius was in no Command Module preparing to go around the limb of the moon, burn his rocket motors and brake into orbit, no, Aquarius was installed in the act of writing about the efforts of other men, his attempts to decipher some first clues to the unvoiced messages of the moon obtained from no more than photographs in color of craters, chains of craters, fields of craters and the moon soil given him through the courtesy of the Manned Spacecraft Center, photographic division of public relations, NASA, yet in the months he worked, the pictures were pored over by him as if he were a medieval alchemist rubbing at a magic stone whose unfelt vibration might yet speak a sweet song to his nerve.

—*Of a Fire on the Moon*

In the book that announced a new era in his literary career, *Advertisements for Myself* (1959), Norman Mailer asserted that "there is finally no way one can try to apprehend complex reality without a 'fiction.' " [1] Mailer, who began his career with the brilliant if derivative naturalistic novel of World War II, *The Naked and the Dead* (1948), has followed that statement with literature marked by a refusal to abandon the goal of dealing with contemporary reality, but at the same time displaying an awareness of the inapplicability of conventional realistic strategies to that task. Part of this literature consists of novels, *An American Dream* (1966) and *Why Are We in Vietnam?* (1967), that explore the subconscious of contemporary American society through the modes of dream and allegory presented within the ostensibly realistic formulas and styles of

35

American popular culture. But Mailer's major course, both in number of works and in impact, has been the direct reportage of public fact. The central point I wish to illustrate in this chapter is that these works, by fusing the external focus of journalism with the internal focus of metafiction, embody a unique solution to the difficulties contemporary writers have experienced in the area of mimesis and interpretation. As an alternative to the limited capacities of realistic fiction, the naive positivism of conventional journalism, or the solipsistic tendencies of fabulation, this strategy affords Mailer a basis from which to directly approach the extreme, often surreal and implausible reality of the postmodern world.

Unlike the fabulators, Mailer has been determined to deal with the great issues and events of the external world in which we all move. But, like them, he has recognized the difficulties presented by the altered reality of that postmodern world. Abandoning the weak author-reader contract of realistic fiction for the strong credibility of journalism, he has nevertheless approached the material of fact with the sophisticated epistemological assumptions of the fabulators. Restricting himself to factual subject matter, he has constructed those facts of the macrocosm in structures assertively and self-consciously fictive, projections of an authorial consciousness actively selecting, interpreting, and shaping those facts within its own microcosm. Because he understands the fiction-making process to be such an inherent part of "reality," Mailer has presented his journalism not only as fiction but also as metafiction, as self-reflexive constructs of consciousness meeting world which may serve as powerful, but necessarily tentative, representations and interpretations of that world.

Mailer's strategy, while so far remaining constant in this basic approach, has varied with his perception of his relation to the events with which he is dealing. It has not always been equally successful. Despite many memorable passages, *Miami and the Siege of Chicago* (1968) is finally rather disappointing as an aesthetic experience because Mailer fails to find a satisfactorily powerful fictive form. As a result, we get something closer to the more traditional interpretive journalism suggested by his subtitle, *An Informal History of the Republican and Democratic Conventions of 1968*. While also having its merits, *Marilyn*

(1973) fails at least partly because, with its almost exclusive dependence on second- or third-hand sources (other biographies) and similarly removed speculation, it fails to establish a credible journalistic contract. The reader finishes *Marilyn* with a vivid sense of Monroe's mystique and Mailer's consciousness, but an uneasy feeling that Mailer has not confronted the actual subject. His best work, in contrast, has been that which has been most resolutely journalistic regarding content, while nevertheless assertively and innovatively fictive in form. The key element in the success of *The Armies of the Night* (1968), *Of a Fire on the Moon* (1970), and *The Executioner's Song* (1979) has been Mailer's selection of a form that best represents his achieved relation to the subject.

I have chosen these three works for extended analysis because I feel that they are the most successfully experimental, certainly the most ambitious and innovative, examples of Mailer's journalistic-metafictional aesthetic in action. The shifting emphases and tactics of Mailer's basic strategy in these three works reflect his differing subjects and changing sense of self. Writing *The Armies of the Night* after leaving the Vietnam protest march on the Pentagon confident of the power of his ideas and personality, Mailer emphasizes the self-conscious manipulation of authorial role and narrative convention; he casts himself as a protagonist able to bridge self and event through action and metaphor. In *Of a Fire on the Moon*, disappointed by his inability, as an earthbound reporter, to capture the meaning of man's first flight to the moon, he responds by presenting Part II as a book about his writing the book on the moon flight through a subsequent process of intense research and imaginative meditation. In *The Executioner's Song*, Mailer makes a radical shift from this focus on the interpretive power of his own consciousness, in response to his feeling that the factual material surrounding Gary Gilmore's execution brought his essential ideas into question. Instead, he has written a book that presents researched fact through the separate perspectives of numerous characters, while at the same time including, as a subject of the text, the interview process through which those perspectives were acquired and which became part of the event. In each of Mailer's journalistic works, the focus on the consciousness of characters as they view facts, rather than on a direct, seemingly objective view of facts, and on the authorial consciousness shaping the overall text, provides an underlying unity to this literature. Mailer's achievement has been to show the possibility—indeed, the power—of literature in dealing with the great events and issues of a world in which even the concept of reality has been doubtful.

The self-conscious strategy by which Mailer foregrounds his concern with form in *The Armies of the Night* is immediately apparent in the subtitle, *History as a Novel/The Novel as History*. This subtitle emphasizes Mailer's division of *The Armies of the Night* into two separate books: Book I, entitled "History as a Novel: The Steps of the Pentagon," and Book II, "The Novel as History: The Battle of the Pentagon." The split nature of the titles themselves suggests the dual level of Mailer's interest in composing this work, for with the first halves Mailer focuses our attention upon his epistemological and aesthetic concerns, while only in the second halves does he bring our attention to the particular subject of a work of journalism. A central theme in *The Armies of the Night* is the problematic relationship between human experience and actual event which leads, in turn, to a problematic relationship between report and event. Mailer thus suggests his concern with presenting different perspectives upon the event by constructing it through different narrative conventions.

Mailer makes these issues explicit in the work itself, both by example and by straightforward commentary. He narrates Book I, "History as a Novel: The Steps of the Pentagon," by far the longer of the two, in the guise of a highly mannered, interpretive and self-conscious authorial persona who performs the part of a contemporary Henry Fielding. Like Fielding, he adopts an ironically superior attitude toward the "comic hero" whom he casts as protagonist ("Mailer," or more precisely Mailer as participant in the event, thus separated by time and role from Mailer as narrator of the event). Also like Fielding, he often intrudes directly into his narrative in order to stop the action temporarily and to discuss his material and his artistic handling of it with the reader. For instance, just after describing Mailer's arrest for transgressing a police line, he pauses:

One of the oldest devices of the novelist—some would call it a vice—is to bring his narrative (after many an excursion) to a pitch of excitement where the reader no matter how cultivated is reduced to a beast who can pant no faster than to ask, "And then what? Then what happens?" At which point the novelist, consummate cruel lover, introduces a digression, aware that delay at this point helps to deepen the addiction of his audience.

This, of course, was Victorian practice. Modern audiences, accustomed to superhighways, put aside their reading at the first annoyance and turn to the television set. So a modern novelist must apologize, even apologize profusely, for daring to leave his narrative, he must in fact absolve himself of the charge of employing a device, he must plead necessity.

So the Novelist now pleads necessity. He will take a momentary delay in the proceedings—because in fact he must—to introduce a further element to our history which will accompany us intermittently to the end.[2]

In using such old-fashioned fictional techniques, Mailer attains the same advantages that fabulators such as Barth and Fowles have won. Parodying fictional conventions, he continues to enjoy the freedoms and perspectives of those conventions, while at the same time constantly reminding the reader that they remain only conventions. Calling himself "the Novelist" and self-consciously using the contrivances of novelistic form, Mailer makes us view the facts of his work as both reliable (in that we are fully shown their source in his firsthand observation) and doubtful (in that we are constantly reminded that they result *merely* from such observation). By insisting that Book I is a history in the form of a novel, Mailer focuses our attention upon the ambiguous and tentative relationship between the actual world and the fictive versions of it, which are all we can know in our individual transforming consciousness.

At the beginning of Book II, "The Novel as History: The Battle of the Pentagon," he explicitly discusses these issues as he justifies the need for a shift in perspective. Referring to narrative convention as a "lens," he suggests that, as a Novelist in Book I, he has provided a "microscope" with which one can "explore the pond" (p. 245). In other words, through his novelistic presentation of the event, he has provided history through the medium of his protagonist's exposed consciousness. That view has been penetrating in depth, but necessarily limited in breadth. At this point he signals the reader that "the Novelist is slowing to a jog, and the Historian is all grip on the rein" (p. 246). In Book II he abandons the advantages of novelistic conventions in favor of those of history, because one needs "a telescope upon a tower if you are scrutinizing the forest" (p. 245). Having provided an interior view of the march as the ambiguous experience of one individual, he now turns to the conventions of the "objective" and external point of view used by the historian in order to portray the march in its panoramic sweep.

Unlike the conventional historian (or journalist), however, Mailer employs the narrative conventions of history in Book II with the same metafictional insistence that they are only conventions—artificial orderings or "fictions"—that he displayed in Book I regarding the conventions of the novel. Reminding the reader that "the instruments of all sciences—history so much as physics—are always constructed in small or large error" (p. 245), he claims that he can now safely employ this inevitably falsifying set of conventions in Book II only because the "crooked" and "warped" lenses of his organizing consciousness have been fully exposed in Book I: "what supports the use of them now is that our intimacy with the master builder of the tower, and the lens grinder of the telescopes (yes, even the machinist of the barrels) has given some advantage for correcting the error of the instruments and the imbalance of his tower. May that be claimed of many histories?" (p. 245). Defining the novel as "the personification of a vision which will enable one to comprehend other visions better" (p. 245), Mailer goes so far as to suggest that a history is really only a different kind of novel, a scope with a different type of lens affording a different view, but necessarily still only a view. The implication is that human consciousness and its products, whether novels or histories, can in their symbolizing process get no closer to any event of the external world than a necessarily imperfect and distorted, but at its best revealing, construct of the author's transforming perceptions.

With this caution set forth, he proceeds to present the overview of the march, including a detailed narrative of its background and events, that one would expect from a conventional work of history. But even knowing that he has provided the particular ordering mechanism that has created the lens of this "history"— the peculiar mixture of philosophy, prejudice, reason, and impulse which make up his consciousness—Mailer the Historian is still not satisfied that the reader has been sufficiently warned of his account's inevitable limitations and distortions. He therefore uses the conventions of historical narrative only while warning the reader of their artifices. Midway through Book II, for instance, he interrupts his narrative to point out the deceptive simplification of even his previous theoretical explanation, arguing that in content the "novel" of Book I has greater claims to history than the "history" of Book II, and that the "history" of Book II is far more fictional, in the popular sense of the term, than Book I:

However, the first book can be, in the formal sense, nothing but a personal history which while written as a novel was to the best of the author's memory scrupulous to facts, and therefore a document; whereas the second, while dutiful to all newspaper accounts, eyewitness reports, and historic inductions available, while even obedient to a general style of historical writing, at least up to this point, while even pretending to be a history (on the basis of its introduction) is finally now to be disclosed as some sort of condensation of a collective novel— which is to admit that an explanation of the mystery of the events at the Pentagon cannot be developed by the methods of history—only by the instincts of the novelist. [p. 284]

Mailer proceeds to enumerate several reasons why this history is actually a novel, including the impossibility of constructing an accurate history from the "chains of false fact" found in journalistic reports of the march, but in essence it is because of the "interior" nature of such an event. The "clearly demarcated limits of historic inquiry" make its conventions inadequate for dealing with the human significance of the march, so Mailer announces that he will transgress them (even as the protagonist "Mailer" transgresses a police line):

So these limits are now relinquished. The collective novel which follows, while still written in the cloak of an historic style, and, therefore, continuously attempting to be scrupulous to the welter of a hundred confusing and opposed facts, will now unashamedly enter that world of strange lights and intuitive speculation which is the novel. Let us, then, fortified by this clarification, this advertisement of intentions, move up to the front, to the six inches of no-man's-land between the U.S. Army and the demonstrators. [pp. 284–85]

Mailer thus argues that even the most scrupulously researched and objectively reported event, if it has any real importance, will in effect be a novel if it in any way approaches truth. (As he later phrased it in *Miami and the Siege of Chicago*, "there is no history without nuance." [3]) This perception is the key to Mailer's approach to journalism: all experience except that limited to meaningless surface inquiry, all knowledge which goes beyond mere gathering of data, is inherently fictional. Mailer's apology for his overtly novelistic approach to journalism is that, by recognizing and admitting this, he is free to exploit its possibilities, while at the same time he keeps the reader aware of the necessarily tentative status of the resulting "truth." Like those metafictionists who work in the realm of the imaginary, Mailer can, in journalism, have his cake and eat it. He can construct a valid order without claiming to represent a single objective scheme. The multiple nature of reality is affirmed even as the "facts" of actuality are dealt with. Mailer is thus able to explore the possible meanings of actual events without confusing the fictive orderings of journalism with the actual events themselves.

Whenever Mailer has centered his journalistic works in the point of view of a character representing the author, his stylistic approach to journalism has been metaphor. This technique is a natural expression of his epistemology, since it openly displays meaning as an individual consciousness's active projection of its ordering and interpretive abilities upon the world around it, abilities in which he has a romantic's confidence. Unlike the symbolic technique with which Capote constructs his supposedly "objective" version of events in *In Cold Blood*, metaphor does not provide the illusion that a particular meaning is inherently present in the world and naturally emanating from it. Metaphor instead presents the act of a mind reaching out to the world in order to *create* meaning, a meaning which is both dynamic and tentative, for it is a construct of active interplay between interior consciousness and external fact. In *In Cold Blood* Capote sees facts as symbols and then portrays them as such; in *The Armies of the Night* Mailer sees a fact, considers any number of possible symbolic values, and then portrays that seeing and consideration. Capote portrays life as significant; Mailer portrays his search for a significance in it. Capote presents actual objects which embody meaning; Mailer presents his attempt to elicit meaning from actual objects, or to project meaning upon them.

A classic instance of this technique in *The Armies of the Night* is Mailer's often-noted and controversial portrayal of the U.S. Marshals whom he observes from a bus as he waits to be taken to jail. In such masterful passages Mailer presents a human consciousness engaged in imaginative observation of physical detail; his writing is reminiscent of Melville's portrayals of Ishmael on the mast-top, before the try-works, and at the task of weaving. This first part of the three-page passage involves a minute scrutiny of the Marshals' faces, which he introduces as follows:

After a while he began to study the Marshals.

Their faces were considerably worse than he had expected. He had had the fortune to be arrested by a man who was incontestably one of the pleasanter Marshals on duty at the Pentagon, he had next met what must be the toughest Marshal in the place—the two had given him a false spectrum. The gang of Marshals now studied outside the bus were enough to firm up any fading loyalty to his own cause: they had the kind of faces which belong to the bad guys in a Western. [p. 171]

Mailer frankly portrays his immediate response to the Marshals by opening the passage with the assertion that "their faces were considerably worse than he had expected," and he quickly stereotypes them by saying that they looked like "bad guys in a Western." By providing these highly subjective generalizations, Mailer establishes overall significance for his impending description of the physical details of their faces, while at the same time warning the reader of the particular bias through which that significance is being interpreted. With this biased perspective exposed, Mailer proceeds with his description:

Some were fat, some were too thin, but nearly all seemed to have those subtle anomalies of the body which come often to men from small towns who have inherited strong features, but end up, by their own measure, in failure. Some would have powerful chests, but abrupt paunches, the skinny ones would have a knob in the shoulder, or a hitch in their gait, their foreheads would have odd cleaving wrinkles, so that one man might look as if an ax had struck him between the eyes, another paid tithe to ten parallel deep lines rising in ridges above his eye brows. The faces of all too many had a low cunning mixed with a stroke of rectitude: if the mouth was slack, the nose was straight and severe; should the lips be tight, the nostrils showed an outsize greed. Many of them looked to be ex-First Sergeants, for they liked to stand with the heels of their hands on the top of their hips, or they had that way of walking, belly forward, which a man will promote when he is in comfortable circumstances with himself and packing a revolver in a belt holster. The toes turn out; the belly struts. [p. 171]

With the key word "seemed" in the first sentence of this descriptive portion of the passage, Mailer both liberates and qualifies the power of his imaginative perception. His coming observations are labeled as interpretive speculations, while at the same time they are freed from the falsifying restraints of neutral recording of fact. He is able to develop his initial stereotyped generalization into a deeper metaphoric identification of the faces with a national spiritual malaise. Quite frankly bringing his consciousness's "fiction" to bear upon the Marshals' physical characteristics, Mailer extends to them a perceived spiritual significance by saying that "all seemed to have those subtle anomalies of the body which come often to men from small towns who have inherited strong features, but end up, by their own measure, in failure." He further extends this idea through such individual figurative descriptions as "another paid tithe to ten parallel deep lines rising in ridges above his eye brows." From these detailed descriptions he at last moves back again to generalizations, both physical and spiritual, as he says that "the faces of all too many had a low cunning mixed with a stroke of rectitude" and "the nostrils showed an outsize greed."

These descriptions are completely intuitive, obviously stereotyped, and no doubt to some degree unfair. Yet they are presented as such. No one could read this passage feeling that he was receiving anything more than Mailer's personal perception of the truth, the power and validity of which the reader is thus free to respond to and evaluate. For this reason the passage is highly suggestive and meaningful journalism—indeed, powerful mimetic and interpretive literature, free from the dangers of the more subtle implications of conventional "objective" journalism, of realistic fiction, or even of Capote's "nonfiction novel."

Having associated the Marshals' faces with the quality of life in American small towns, thereby introducing the thematic motif that such life moves from initial promise to eventual despair, Mailer returns to this enlarging interpretation with his observations of their features:

They were older men than he might have expected, some in their late thirties, more in their forties, a few looked to be over fifty, but then that may have been why they were here to receive prisoners rather than out on the line—in any case they emitted a collective spirit which, to his mind, spoke of little which was good, for their eyes were blank and dull, that familiar small-town cast of eye which speaks of apathy rising to fanaticism only to subside in apathy again. [p. 171]

This concluding generalization turns out to be only a transition into still more general and abstract intuitive speculations upon the Marshals' significance. With a parenthesis which exposes one of the preconceptions with which he has approached the Marshals, he again elaborates upon his notions concerning small-town life, emphasizing the tentative status of these perceptions as partly the products of long-considered opinions: "(Mailer had wondered more than once at that curious demand of small-town life which leaves something good and bright in the eyes of some, is so deadening for others—it was his impression that people in small towns had eyes which were generally livelier or emptier than the more concentrated look of city vision.)"

With the parenthetical preconceptions displayed, Mailer returns to the Marshals:

These Marshals had the dead eye and sour cigar, that sly shuffle of propriety and rut which so often comes out in a small-town sheriff as patriotism and the sweet stink of a crooked dollar. Small-town sheriffs sidled over to a crooked dollar like a High Episcopalian hooked on a closet queen. If one could find the irredeemable madness of America (for we are a nation where weeds will breed in the gilding tank) it was in those later afternoon race track faces coming into the neon lights of the parimutuel windows, or those early morning hollows in the eye of the soul in places like Vegas where the fevers of America go livid in the hum of the night, and Grandmother, the churchgoer, orange hair burning bright now crooned over the One-Arm Bandit, pocketbook open, driving those half-dollars home, home to the slot. [p. 172]

At this point an ontological change has taken place. Stanley T. Gutman has pointed out that, in Mailer's novel *An American Dream*, "the metaphorical description becomes an essential part of the reality Mailer describes." [4] The same is true in this journalistic passage from *The Armies of the Night*. The spiritual significance which Mailer previously suggested and developed through metaphor has now been compressed into a strongly connotative physical description of the Marshals. They have "the dead eye," "sour cigar," and "sly shuffle." The metaphorical linkages between observed features and imaginative interpretation have at this point merged into imaginative description; the observed facts and interpretive speculations have become one. Yet these products of metaphor now serve as concrete components, to be linked with new and more daring speculations in further extending metaphors. "The dead eye and sour cigar, that sly shuffle" become images of that "propriety and rut which so often comes out in a small-town sheriff as patriotism and the sweet stink of a crooked dollar." We have moved back to the small town, but with added abstractions which lead us out now to broad speculation upon "the irredeemable madness of America." We have no sooner reached this broad abstraction than it is compressed back into a new image and character, a fantasy creature of Mailer's consciousness, the "Grandma with Orange Hair" who serves as the title character of the chapter.

In this descriptive passage, in a work that is most generally called "documentary" or "nonfiction," Mailer proceeds to take this imagined character and portray her in a fully realized surrealist fantasy, complete with dialogue:

"Madame, we are burning children in Vietnam."
"Boy, you just go get yourself lost. Grandma's about ready for a kiss from the jackpot."
The burned child is brought into the gaming hall on her hospital bed.
"Madame, regard our act in Vietnam."
"I hit! I hit! Hot deedy, I hit. Why, you poor burned child—you just brought me luck. Here, honey, here's a lucky half-dollar in reward. And listen sugar, tell the nurse to change your sheets. Those sheets sure do

stink. I hope you ain't got gangrene. Hee hee, hee hee. I get a supreme pleasure mixing with gooks in Vegas."

One did not have to look for who would work in the concentration camps and the liquidation centers—the garrison would be filled with applicants from the pages of a hundred American novels, from *Day of the Locust* and *Naked Lunch* and *The Magic Christian*, one could enlist half the Marshals outside this bus, simple, honest, hard-working government law-enforcement agents, yeah! There was something at loose now in American life, the poet's beast slinking to the marketplace. [p. 172]

With this allusion to American absurdist novels to expand on his view of the Marshals (he had earlier made a possible allusion to his own *The Naked and the Dead* when he said that they looked like ex-First Sergeants), Mailer uses his elaborate metaphorical base to launch into an extended meditation upon America's history, present condition, and future. This meditation is itself presented through a metaphor, as America is portrayed as a body whose fever has "left the blood" to go into "the cells," thus setting off a cancerous madness of growth responsible for all of the manifestations of contemporary American life, from the "shopping centers" to the wars in foreign lands:

The country had always been wild. It had always been harsh and hard, it had always had a fever—when life in one American town grew insupportable, one could travel, the fever to travel was in the American blood, so said all, but now the fever had left the blood, it was in the cells, the cells traveled, and the cells were as insane as Grandma with orange hair. The small towns were disappearing in the bypasses and the supermarkets and the shopping centers, the small town in America was losing its sense of the knuckle, the herb, and the root, the walking sticks were no longer cut from trees, nor were they cured, the schools did not have crazy old teachers now but teaching aids, and in the libraries, *National Geographic* gave way to *TV Guide*. Enough of the old walled town had once remained in the American small town for gnomes and dwarfs and knaves and churls (yes, and owls and elves and crickets) to live in the constellated cities of the spiders below the eaves in the old leaning barn which—for all one knew—had been a secret ear to the fevers of the small town, message center for the inhuman dreams which passed through the town at night in sleep and came to tell their insane tale of the old barbarian lust to slaughter villages and drink their blood, yes who knew which ghosts, and which crickets, with which spider would commune—which prayers and whose witch's curses would travel those subterranean trails of the natural kingdom about the town, who knows which fevers were forged in such communion and returned on the blood to the seed, it was an era when the message came by the wind and not by the wire (for the town gossip began to go mad when the telephone tuned its buds to the tip of her tongue) the American small town grew out of itself, and grew out of itself again and again, harmony between communication and the wind, between lives and ghosts, insanity, the solemn reaches of nature where insanity could learn melancholy (and madness some measure of modesty) had all been lost now, lost to the American small town. It had grown out of itself again and again, its cells traveled, worked for government, found security through wars in foreign lands, and the nightmares which passed on the winds in the old small towns now traveled on the nozzle tip of the flame thrower, no dreams now of barbarian lusts, slaughtered villages, battles of blood, no, nor any need for them—technology had driven insanity out of the wind and out of the attic, and out of all the lost primitive places: one had to find it now wherever fever, force, and machines could come together, in Vegas, at the race track, in pro football, race riots for the Negro, suburban orgies—none of it was enough—one had to find it in Vietnam; that was where the small town had gone to get its kicks.

That was on the faces of the Marshals. [pp. 172–74]

Portraying American history as a cancer cell which has traveled from the small town to the "nozzle tip of the flame-thrower," Mailer at last attains his imaginative insight (one which his previous book, *Why Are We in Vietnam?*, shows he had all along). The combination of America's new technology and its oldest impulses results inevitably in destruction. With the possibilities and mysteries which Americans had originally sought in this new land now eliminated, contemporary Americans have found perverted versions of them in contemporary fragmentation and apocalypse.

When Mailer finally brings this three-page passage to an abrupt end with the assertion, "That was on the faces of the Marshals," he jars us into realizing both the power and tenuousness of this product of the human consciousness. He goes on to admit that "it was a great deal to read on the limited evidence before him," but he justifies his intuitive flight by telling us that he knew similar faces in the army twenty years before.[5] Yet no sooner has he offered this self-support based on personal experience than he is off into speculation again, using this experience as basis for further meditation on the national significance of the changes in the two sets of faces over those twenty years.

This passage offers a few observed "facts." We see them transformed through the metaphoric process into images charged with significant nuance; we see those metaphoric products used as the concrete elements of yet more daring metaphors which are then expanded into a complete scene of surreal fantasy, and then enlarged into a nearly stream-of-consciousness disquisition on the history and future of America. For all his blatant stereotyping and prejudice, Mailer has powerfully dramatized possible truth. Yet Mario Puzo, for one, has asked the pertinent question: "Are these the same Marshals who fought to get Meredith into Old Miss?" [6]

This is the kind of qualification Mailer's journalism demands. However, I think his work does not finally stand or fall on the *objective* truth of his insights, any more than does Melville's through the perceiving, meditative consciousness of Ishmael in *Moby-Dick*. Mailer has hardly claimed to be objective; he presents his perceptions as perceptions, though ones attained through extraordinary acts of observation and imagination. And a crucial value of such passages is the experiencing of the process of a human consciousness interacting profoundly with an actual event, wrestling with its various "facts" in an intense effort to break through to an understanding of the fact and of the self. In *The Armies of the Night* Mailer has adapted to journalism the fictional innovations of such authors as Melville and Joyce in the depiction of a human consciousness (that of "Mailer" the protagonist) in the act of apprehending the world, even while presenting that consciousness in the ironic framework of a Fielding-like authorial narrator. In doing so he has convincingly communicated the meanings and shapes discernible in the media events of the contemporary landscape. Perhaps even more important, he has attempted to portray the process of a significant engagement with such events. Laura Adams has emphasized that Mailer's primary aesthetic and theme in all of his literature is growth.[7] Growth is the ultimate subject and method of scenes such as his imaginative observation of the Marshals' faces.

After parts appeared initially in *Life* magazine,[8] *Of a Fire on the Moon* was published in 1970 to a decidedly mixed critical reception. A major criticism has been that the book is the rather pathetic result of Mailer's confrontation with a subject beyond his abilities, a subject into which he was unfortunately trapped by the demands of a million-dollar contract and his overwhelming ego. This view is rather typically represented by Roger Sale's assertion that "here, where he really has very little to say about what is happening, we are left, often quite embarrassed, with a technique that suddenly makes Mailer seem a driveler and a show."[9] It is true that Mailer could not go to the moon in the Apollo space capsule, and that he could not even gain personal interviews with the three astronauts who made the trip or be on the recovery ship to observe their return. But to properly experience *Of a Fire on the Moon* one must engage the book on its own terms—as an *imaginative counterpart* to its subject, rather than as a simple representation of it.

Faced with an event which seems as unreportable as it is significant, Mailer chooses not to disguise the weakness of his position; rather, he sees it as a challenge that makes up the true dramatic subject of his book. As a result, the frank recognition of artifice becomes even more important as message and method in *Of a Fire on the Moon* than it was in *The Armies of the Night*. Alfred Kazin is correct in his perception (though I think less so in his disapproving implication) that *Of a Fire on the Moon* is "a book about a novelist trying to write instant history."[10] In *Of a Fire on the Moon*, as in his previous works, we have Mailer as narrator presenting Mailer as protagonist (called "Aquarius" here, rather than the "Mailer" of *The Armies of the Night* or the "reporter" of *Miami and the Siege of Chicago*) engaged in a heroic struggle with an event; but in this work the central dramatic struggle is the protagonist's attempt to transform the event into his book. By composing *Of a Fire on the Moon* as a book about writing *Of a Fire on the Moon*, Mailer portrays the macrocosmic world of journalism within the microcosm of his authorial consciousness. Rather than a mere literary game, this is a self-conscious assertion of the need to bring the world of fiction to a factual event—that is, to re-create and explore an event in one's consciousness until a meaningful shape and substance are discovered. Mailer adopts the methods of metafiction as a way of moving beyond the facts of journalism into the realm of truth, of pattern and interpretation, while always keeping the central role of his consciousness in this process before the reader.

In Part I, which he entitles "Aquarius" and presents from the perspective of firsthand but distant observation, Mailer establishes this structure by stressing Aquarius' growing fear that this subject is beyond his capabilities, and expressing his eventual perception of why and how he must deal with it. Indicating that he finds the Apollo mission particularly ill suited to his character and methods as a journalist ("It would be as easy to go to the Amazon to study moon rocks as to write a book about these space matters, foreign to him, which everyone would agree is worth a million dollars"),[11] he repeatedly presents aspects of the subject that are beyond his previous concepts, beyond even his power to conceive.[12] He listens to the astronauts at the pre-flight press conference; they speak a "technologese" which he feels is an attempt to sublimate dread by reducing the significance of their actions. They seem to Mailer to embody a movement by the WASP culture to impose a predetermined pattern and a totalitarian narrowness of vision. And at the Houston Space Center, surrounded by the new technology, he feels that he is being replaced: " 'Recognize,' the windowless walls say, 'that something is taking over from you, kid' " (p. 14).

Soon, however, he begins to consider the possibility that the new reality being opened by technology is demanding a similar creative thrust from him. After hearing the astronaut Neil Armstrong discuss his boyhood dream of "hovering," and having decided that the flight to the moon has for mankind the significance of a dream, Mailer shows himself deciding that he can write this book, that indeed it might be an artistic challenge of heroic scope that could result in "a work whose size might relieve the chore" (p. 48). Later he suggests that this work is itself becoming a dream-like flight as he contemplates "the size of the feat and the project before him, and by the night before the launch, he was already in orbit himself, a simple fellow with a mind which idled agreeably, his mind indeed out in some weightless trip through the vacuum of a psychic space . . ." (pp. 56–57). By the time Mailer draws Part I to a close, the astronauts are back on earth and Mailer has reported the entire mission from the scene at Houston and Cape Kennedy; nevertheless, he perceives his work of journalism as only having begun, for he knows that both the facts and the meaning of this subject have eluded him. Convinced that the trip is part of some "monumental vision" of either God or the Devil,[13] he ends the description of the Apollo flight in Part I with the beginning of his own journey, describing himself as "ready to head for home, the writing of a book and conceivably the pouring of a drink. The study of more than one technical manual awaited him" (p. 152).

Far more densely factual and yet more boldly imaginative than Part I, Part II—entitled "Apollo"—is the crucial center of Mailer's metafictional structure. It is a portrayal of Aquarius sitting at his writing desk and attempting to create a *meaningful* flight to the moon, a verbal construct which will parallel the Apollo mission's triumph of measure with a triumph of metaphor. Many readers have missed this framework of Part II and have mistakenly assumed that Aquarius is altogether absent from it. This misconception has probably resulted from Mailer's concentration on a meticulous description of the flight instead of on his usual self-dramatization, but at various key points in the narrative he directly alludes to his position and function. After concluding Part I with his journey home to write the book, he begins Part II by declaring that he is about to retell the events of Part I, on the assumption that "the story steeped in further detail has become something like another account even as a day recaptured in a dream has acquired the reality of a more extraordinary day" (p. 155). He introduces Section x of the first chapter of Part II with the words "as Aquarius continued to write in later days and weeks, and then in the months after Apollo 11 lifted off from the pad at Cape Kennedy and began its trip to the moon . . ." (p. 208). He interrupts the superbly realized illusion of actuality in his description of the astronauts' orbiting view of the surface of the dark side of the moon by reminding the reader that the author is "staring down on a photograph" (p. 300). These authorial references to the self keep the reader aware that Part II is not a mere account of, but an actual re-creation of the flight, his consciousness's artificial but profound experience of external fact.

The importance which Mailer places upon the reader experiencing Part II as Aquarius' construct of researched fact and imaginative participation is apparent in his correction, in a later paperback edition, of a factual error that appears in the original hardbound book. He had described the Eagle descending to the lunar surface "in a murk of dust and sunlight and landing lights" (p. 381). Rather than ignoring or removing the error in the paperback, he lets the description stand but adds a footnote: "Mr. Earle E. Spamer corrects this point by informing me there are no landing lights on the LEM. Lights on 'is to indicate that the 60-seconds-of-fuel-remaining light' has just gone on." [14] This combination of erroneous narration and corrective footnote suggests that the landing and, implicitly, the entire Apollo mission now have a dual ontological status—that of the actual events, and that of Mailer's fictive construct of them. Changes in his knowledge of the former can only be *appended* to the latter; valid in terms of the macrocosmic reality of the actual events, they stand somehow outside the validity of the microcosmic reality of Mailer's narrative version.

In his retelling of the astronauts' landing and walk on the moon, Mailer makes his most daring attempt to fuse the actuality of the Apollo mission with his imaginative participation. As always, his central assumption is the necessity of artifice and his crucial technique metaphor. He prefaces the account with an assertion of its absolute factuality, acknowledging that if he is to "travel into the inner space of his brain to uncover the mysteries of the moon, he could dignify that expedition only if he obeyed the irritatingly modest data of the given, the words, the humor, and resolute lack of poetic immortality in the astronauts' communications with the earth. . ." (p. 293). Mailer does indeed hold to the banal facts of the astronauts' words and behavior while on the moon, but by imaginatively projecting himself through metaphor into their places, he is able to make his own voyage at his writing desk.

In subsequent chapters Mailer succeeds, through his intensive research and imaginative projection, in constructing an account which is far more informative, dramatic, and significant than the one he presented in Part I. Because the events are immersed in technology and the language of technology, they seem banal if only reported. But while he at times seems to be straining, Mailer penetrates this barrier in such a way that the reader can perceive the facts as elements of a true drama. Consider, for example, his presentation of the instant when Armstrong and Aldrin first attempted to re-dock with Apollo 11. Having prepared the reader with extensive information on the two men's previous brushes with death in technological mishaps, he composes a scene that reveals suspense and significance:

Just before that moment "all hell broke loose." It was Collins' remark, there on the transcript, but he has no recollection of saying it. As he fired the charges, there was an abrupt, shocking and "abnormal" oscillation. The ships began to yaw from side to side at a rapid rate. What an instant for Armstrong—did the memory of the sun flashing through the window of Gemini 8 come back to him? What a thunder for Aldrin after the mishaps with the computer on the day before, what a stroke of doubt for Collins at where the mistake could be. "All hell broke loose." Hell was when the unforeseen insisted on emerging. Shivering and quivering, the ships slapped from side to side. [p. 429]

Of course, this scene, like others, depends not only on his research, but also on his intuitive knowledge of how he is sure it *must* have felt. The role of his imagination is not disguised. Indeed, Mailer continually asserts it through the most obvious metaphorical additions of his own concepts. A climactic instance is his description of Armstrong's view as he goes to sleep in the capsule after man's first moon-walk: "In front of his face was the eyepiece of the telescope. The earth was in its field of view, and the earth 'like a big blue eyeball' stared back at him. They could not sleep. Like the eye of a victim just murdered, the earth stared back at him" (p. 413). By first quoting Armstrong's own personifying simile for his reaction to the earth's appearance, and then adding his own simile, Mailer is able to transform Armstrong's benign version of the moment into a profoundly disturbing one. For Mailer, man's having walked on the moon, an orb which his previous books show has long had profound significance for him,[15] is the transgression of a taboo which necessarily kills an entire reality. Man is now in the future, and the new reality is not yet known. The astronauts would deny any such troubling significance; by imaginatively projecting himself into their shoes and metaphorically taking the flight, Mailer is able to insist on it.

Mailer constructs Part III, "The Age of Aquarius," as the search of its author-protagonist for an ending, a final meaning, to the book and its subject. He opens it, as he did the previous two parts, with a metafictional discussion and justification of his aims and methods. Arguing that a fair judge is one who "travels through his own desolations before passing sentence" and "to write was to judge" (pp. 435–36), he will have to consider his own activities during the expiring decade before he can offer a valid verdict on the moon flight's significance. Mailer then proceeds to narrate Part III as an account of his experience in Provincetown, Massachusetts, during the summer when he struggled to complete the book. He frankly shows how the mental confrontation with the moon flight is influencing his experience with his surroundings (he finds himself disgusted with the indulgent life of the "Hip" now that he contemplates the astronauts' triumph), and how, in turn, that experience is affecting his view of the moon flight's significance.

He presents the ending of Part III as a dramatization of the time when he stood in Houston before the glass-encased moon rock brought back by the astronauts. Mailer ends the book with this scene because the rock functions perfectly as the end product of the astronauts' actual voyage and of Mailer's literary voyage:

it came on the day he stood in quiet before that object from the moon, that rock which gave him certitude enough to know he would write his book and in some part applaud the feat and honor the astronauts . . . yes, we might have to go out into space until the mystery of new discovery would force us to regard the world once again as poets, behold it as savages who knew that if the universe was a lock, its key was metaphor rather than measure.

Marvelous little moon rock. What the Devil did it say? [p. 471]

As the astronauts' attainment, the moon rock is fact; as Mailer's, it is a metaphor. Whereas the astronauts have forever changed the world, Mailer has succeeded in creating some sense of the possibility and meaning of that change, has even perhaps contributed to it himself. Feeling deeply his Hip friends' distaste for the predetermined pattern and narrow vision of the astronauts' quest, sensing the utter banality of the quality of their experience, he has nevertheless recognized the apocalyptic significance of the astronauts' triumph and has responded to it through a quest of his own.

In such works as *The Armies of the Night* and *Of a Fire on the Moon*, Mailer has avoided the illusory separation of consciousness and event inherent in conventional journalism and realistic fiction. By writing about media events as imaginative experiences of his self, Mailer can penetrate their complexities and ambiguities so that they become comprehensible for the individual without becoming falsified by stereotype and formula. By using the stylistic and structural methods of metaphor and metafiction, he can probe the meanings of events while insuring that his imaginative constructions are experienced as such by his readers, and can avoid letting them appear to be simple representations of objective fact. Through his innovative combination of a journalistic contract and experimental fictional technique, Mailer found, in the 1960's, an unusually secure position from which to deal with a period in which experience seemed to escape so many writers.

The Executioner's Song, a thousand-page account of the life and death of Gary Gilmore, is in many ways a remarkable shift in Mailer's journalism. While the book was received very favorably, scarcely a reviewer attempted to hide his astonishment at Mailer's having produced a work of journalism in which "Mailer" or "Aquarius" is neither a protagonist nor even a visible narrator, and in which the baroque stylistic texture of complex metaphor and allusion is abandoned for a prose so spare as to suggest Hemingway or even conventional reportage. These differences reflect, I think, both Mailer's capacity for change and growth as an artist and the catalyst that new material acquired through journalistic methods can provide for such artistic transformation. Yet, in the reviewers' understandable surprise at the withdrawal of the Mailer persona, the elements of continuity with Mailer's previous journalism have gone largely unnoticed. Those elements now stand, if anything, in sharper relief: what clearly remains is Mailer's emphasis on the necessity of fiction for the apprehension of complex reality, and thus the need for a self-reflexive assertion of authorial role and a correlating presentation of fact through consciousness.

Mailer has chosen, in this most reportorial of his works—and in contrast to Capote's claims in similar circumstances to having achieved a "nonfiction novel"—to assert in the afterword and on the book jacket that it is a "true life novel." (Of the new journalistic works discussed in this study, it is the only one listed as fiction by the Library of Congress, and has been placed in that category on best-seller lists.) This presentation of the book as essentially fiction despite its factual content is, as we have seen in this and the preceding chapter, consistent with Mailer's previous theoretical comments. The "old prison rhyme" that he provides as epigraph and epitaph serves to further emphasize the fictive frame of reference of the invisible yet ever-present author. Only two pages after so labeling this verse for the second time, Mailer exposes it in his afterword as such only in the sense of a fictional conceit: "Finally, one would confess one's creations. The *old prison rhyme* at the beginning and end of this book is not, alas, an ancient ditty but a new one, and was written by this author ten years ago for his movie *Maidstone*." [16] Mailer presents the reader with an emphatically journalistic reality for 1,050 pages of reportorial narrative, only to then turn about with a whimsical "alas" and admit to the fictive element that necessarily "frames" a report, an element that can be disguised but never eliminated. Calling the reader's attention to the inevitably transforming role of his fiction-making consciousness, he reminds the reader that his work, despite its factual content, is in the ultimate epistemological and ontological sense an artifice, an aesthetic shape that necessarily achieves mimesis of the external world through the constructing act of a shaping consciousness.

At the same time, "An Afterword" functions as a kind of second ending to the book, one strangely without and within the text. Outside the narrative, outside the fictional frame set up by the "old prison rhyme," outside the portentous FINIS that places a seemingly final boundary after the rhyme, the afterword comes as a rather terse answer to a quiet mystery that the narrative has gradually and insistently brought to the forefront of the reader's mind: how did this narrative come to be made? Mailer creates this metafictional layer of experience for the reader by focusing in Book Two on the efforts of interviewers, particularly Lawrence Schiller, to gather the material that clearly made possible the narrative we are reading. Indeed, Mailer spends so much of Book II dramatizing the various motivations, high and low, of Schiller that the chief researcher of *The Executioner's Song* serves a function very close to that of "Mailer" and "Aquarius" in previous works. Mailer goes so far as to include portions of interviews on which earlier scenes were partially based, revealing, in the last such printed transcript, the unpleasant probing, seducing, and even violating nature of much of Schiller's interviewing that has led to the intimate scenes which the author has created and in which the reader has voyeuristically participated (pp. 1040–42).

Indeed, the text of Book II develops simultaneously on two planes of interest in a mirror-like relation. The explicit subject of the book is the execution of the central character, culminating in the autopsy in which his body is finally dissected so that its separate parts may be used or examined. The second, metafictional subject, the making of the book, climaxes in Mailer's afterword; there it, too, having been proclaimed FINIS, is opened for examination of its working parts (the sources, methods of documentation and selection, devices, etc.). The ultimate power of aesthetic form is silently asserted, for both the character Gilmore and the text itself survive their termination and subsequent autopsy, living on in our consciousness as a result of the strength of the fictional creation that is the text.

Mailer's metafictional devices in *The Executioner's Song* or any of his other journalistic works emphasize the fiction-making process in our apprehension of "reality." That emphasis frees him to use his mimetic and interpretive powers with an awareness of their tentative nature. The subjects and concerns of *The Executioner's Song* clearly place it in the tradition of the great social and political novels of Dreiser, Dos Passos and Farrell. The text bears out Mailer's assertion that the huge new body of "invaluable material" he found in Lawrence Schiller's interviews caused him to become "fascinated at a certain point in drawing an objective picture of American society using the thread of the story." [17] He has also said that he thought the "true title" for the book was "American Virtue," because he discovered in writing it that a concern with doing "the right thing," however varying the concept of what that might entail, was the trait most characteristic of Americans. (He gave up the title because he was convinced that it would be interpreted as "sardonic." [18]) This concern with a mimetic and interpretive portrayal of American society contrasts sharply with the elaborate word and plot games of the other big book published at almost the same time, John Barth's fabulist metafiction *Letters*. And Mailer's secret title similarly suggests the sharp difference in his subjects and themes from those of Thomas Pynchon when it is compared to "Mindless Pleasures," the working title of *Gravity's Rainbow*, perhaps *the* big book of fabulist writing.

But while *The Executioner's Song* belongs, in its subject, to the tradition of the social and political novels of the realists and naturalists, Mailer is now too far removed from the philosophical premises of those works to merely organize new material according to their forms and themes. He is also acutely aware that the contemporary role of the media, including that of the book's sources, is a reality-distorting element that cannot be ignored in documenting a "media event" without falsifying the reality of the event still further. The metafictional aspects of *The Executioner's Song*, in combination with the factual author-reader contract, exist to avoid the positivist assumptions and deny the explanatory theories of its most obvious predecessors. Through those aspects Mailer asserts that the book is both his personal creation and a researched document, not a disguised use of material to present a single point of view. By combining the epistemological sophistication and self-examination of metafiction with the factual credibility of journalism, Mailer restores mimetic power to the novel.

Mailer's shift in *The Executioner's Song* away from the Mailer-protagonist and the metaphorical style of his previous journalism reflects his desire to present a mass of new material that was more important in the questions it posed than in any answers he had available. Mailer has been very explicit about his reasons for this shift in emphasis from interpretation to mimesis:

. . . what I discovered at a certain point—and I think this is really the core of it—is I thought, I can write a book that will really make people think in a way they haven't quite thought before. This material made me begin to look at ten or 20 serious questions in an altogether new fashion, and it made me humble in that I just didn't know the answers. I mean, I've had the habit for years of feeling that I could dominate any question pretty quickly—it's been my vanity. And it was an exceptional experience to spend all these months and find that gently but inevitably, I was finding myself in more profound—not confusion—but doubt about my ability to answer to give definitive answers to these questions. But what I had instead is that I was collecting materials that I would think about for the rest of my life. In other words, I was getting new experience. I thought it might be very nice for once just to write a book which doesn't have answers, but poses delicate questions with a great deal of evidence and a great deal of material and let people argue over it. I feel there are any number of areas in this book where there are people who have better answers to give than I have.[19]

Mailer did not cast "Mailer" or "Aquarius" as his protagonist because for once he felt that the journalistic subject was truly out of reach of his interpretive powers, not bridgeable by the metaphorical constructions of himself as either observer or author. But Mailer's putting aside a particular protagonist and stylistic device did not involve turning away from the central tenets of his journalistic aesthetic as defined by works up to that time. Like *The Armies of the Night* and *Of a Fire on the Moon*, and in distinct contrast to Capote's *In Cold Blood*, all the material in *The Executioner's Song*—with the exception of documents such as newspaper stories, interview transcripts, and letters—is presented through an individual consciousness; more precisely, through a consciousness filtered through yet a second consciousness. Just as Mailer emphasizes the fictional quality of his work, in contrast to Capote's claim that *In Cold Blood* is a "nonfiction novel," he also carefully admits in the afterword that, despite his great efforts at accuracy, "this does not mean it has come a great deal closer to the truth than the recollections of the witnesses" (p. 1051).

Capote manipulates point of view and supplies information in *In Cold Blood* with little apparent regard for their original correlation,[20] and he narrates the book as an omniscient narrator very often external to the consciousness of any of the characters, thus seeming to provide direct, objective views of settings and events. Most reviewers felt that Mailer had adopted this omniscient, objective technique in *The Executioner's Song*. Actually, the book is always narrated by an authorial voice looking through a character's consciousness in an ambiguous technique, most often associated with impressionist authors, that leaves the consciousness of the author and character at times fused, at times separate, often not quite clearly either.

In regard to point of view and style, the primary difference between *The Armies of the Night* and *The Executioner's Song* is the difference between the protagonist-consciousness of Mailer and the lesser-character multiple consciousness of Brenda Nicol, Bessie Gilmore, Nicole Baker, Lawrence Schiller, as well as the many others, from Mormon lawyers to prison informers, through whom Mailer narrates. It is the difference between an authorial persona romantically confident of the power of his philosophical ideas and one humbly fascinated by his discovery of new material and impenetrable questions. Mailer thus shifts from a ruminating author to a quiet one, and from a character who perceives through profound metaphor to a mass of characters each of whom perceives through a consciousness formed by unique experience and culturally received ideas. In both *The Armies of the Night* and *The Executioner's Song* the central subject is this engagement of consciousness and world. But in the latter the author takes us on a tour of American society, focused by the phenomenon of Gary Gilmore, through the consciousness of a mass of diverse characters. This consciousness is the true subject of Mailer's mimesis.

As he shifts from one point of view to another in *The Executioner's Song*, Mailer shifts to the salient aspects of the different characters' language while retaining an overall consistency in the spare, loose rhythms of the prose. He almost completely avoids making any direct, clearly identifiable authorial comment. Occasionally, as in the two passages below, the possibility of such comment exists, though it is not clear whether he is the source of the thought, or only of its selection and phrasing:

With all the excitement, Brenda was hardly taking into account that it was practically the same route their Mormon great-grandfather took when he jumped off from Missouri with a handcart near to a hundred years ago, and pushed west with all he owned over the prairies, and the passes of the Rockies, to come to rest at Provo in the Mormon Kingdom of Deseret just fifty miles below Salt Lake. [p. 10]

Brenda took a good look into his eyes and felt full of sadness again. His eyes had the expression of rabbits she had flushed, scared-rabbit was the common expression, but she had looked into those eyes of scared rabbits and they were calm and tender and kind of curious. They did not know what would happen next. [p. 16]

In the first passage it is not clear whether Brenda, Gilmore's cousin, later recognized an irony when she realized the parallel between her great-grandfather's journey and Gilmore's; or whether she later realized the parallel, but Mailer has stylistically added his own ironic implication; or whether he himself provides the ironic parallel without her realization of it at all. In the second passage the perceptions are all clearly identified as Brenda's until the final sentence, which is Mailer's often-stated definition of an existential situation. It is not clear whether Mailer is reporting Brenda's articulation of the expression in Gilmore's eyes, or whether he is articulating what he believes she is indicating by her reported observations and comparisons, or whether he is adding his own portentous interpretation to the character's relatively banal perception. Clearly Mailer's authorial presence is pervasive, though considerably more ambiguous and restrained than in his previous journalism. In such passages the authorial point of view seems to emerge slightly, without ever quite separating from that of the character. Mailer's technique here, in contrast to the metaphors in *Of a Fire on the Moon*, with which he obtrusively adds his own interpretations to the banal views of the astronauts, suggests an articulation of meaning and import inherent in the characters' perceptions. The reader is always aware that he is looking at facts through an authorial consciousness—looking at, and through, a character's consciousness.

Mailer also makes his authorial presence felt through a silently obtrusive use of short paragraphs set off at frequent intervals with extra space. This unusual compositional technique makes the text seem both more documentary like, imitating the effect of snapshots, and more poetic, adding a quiet variation in emphasis and import to seemingly banal conversation. These effects are evident in the following passage, excerpted from the scene in which Gilmore's cousin is driving to the airport with her husband to pick up the just-released convict she has agreed to sponsor. Although they have corresponded throughout his imprisonment, she hasn't seen him since they were childhood playmates:

On the ride, Brenda kept telling John to hurry up. It was the middle of the night, and nobody was on the road. John, however, wasn't about to get a ticket. They were traveling the Interstate, after all. So he kept at 60. Brenda gave up fighting. She was altogether too excited to fight.

"Oh, my God," said Brenda, "I wonder how tall he is."
"What?" said Johnny.

She had begun to think he might be short. That would be awful. Brenda was only five feet five, but it was a height she knew well. From the time she was ten years old, she had been 130 pounds, five-five, and wholly equipped with the same size bra as now—C cup.
"What do you mean, is he tall?" asked Johnny.
"I don't know, I hope he is."

In junior high, if she put on heels, the only person big enough to dance with her was the gym teacher. She used to hate like hell to kiss a boy on the forehead and tell him good night. In fact, she got so paranoid about being tall it could have stunted her growth.
It certainly made her like boys taller than herself. They let her feel feminine. She just had this nightmare that when they got to the airport, Gary would only come up to her armpit. Why, she would abandon the whole thing right there. Shift for yourself, she would tell him. [p. 11]

Mailer blends the consciousness of Brenda, conveyed through her thoughts and characteristic language, with his own authorial observation and interpretation, conveyed through the focus and emphasis of selection and spacing. The result is a report not only of the scene but, most importantly and quite subtly, of the activities of Brenda's consciousness during this scene, with suggestions even of her unconscious. Brenda's actions in seeking Gilmore's release and the cautious but generous cooperation of her husband are portrayed by Mailer as essentially very noble in motivation—the desire to help a troubled family member return to a useful and happy life. But in the above passage and in the scenes from which it is lifted, Mailer suggests the presence of another level of experience: Brenda's sexual attraction to the idea of a man who clearly embodies a life less safe and orderly than that embodied by her husband.

The quiet nature of Mailer's focus and commentary probably gives the conflict a greater verisimilitude than more overt devices would. It seems essentially to be a conflict between the surface motivations of a rational, social world and the more secret, only half-recognized and partially admitted desires of the irrational, private world of the unconscious. The result is a strong underlying tension created by viewing a character driven by motivations of which she is aware, without quite allowing herself to admit them. This foreshadows a conflict that Gilmore's presence in the Mormon community will represent, and the larger symbolic significance that may be perceived in that conflict for the nation: the one between its public ideals and the "sub-terranean river of untapped ferocious, lonely and romantic desires, that concentration of ecstasy and violence which is the dream life of the nation," [21] which has obsessed Mailer throughout his career. In this way *The Executioner's Song* explores the same subject and theme as *An American Dream*. But here Mailer is able to explore that deep psychological division in the national consciousness through the mimetic form of a journalistic report, with the unique power such a report holds on the reader's credibility.

Capote attempted and achieved a similar transformation of journalistic subject into larger mythic significance. *In Cold Blood*, however, ultimately falls short of *The Executioner's Song* in its credibility and its thematic implications. The weakness of Capote's book lies in its rather rigid adherence to traditional forms. While Capote claimed to have written a nonfiction novel, he manipulated his facts with an omniscient authority and interpretively motivated freedom that raises serious doubts about the book's factual and thematic status. Determined to make the book assume the form of a traditional novel, he apparently placed facts in a consciousness in which he had chosen to locate the point of view of certain scenes, when the facts of those scenes had actually been derived from other sources. (Mailer instead shifts from one point of view to another in apparently strict correlation to his interviews, admitting in the afterword to the one exception.) Capote left himself out of events in which he actually had a considerable role. (Mailer, in contrast, focuses in Book Two on the presence, motivations, and methods of the interviewers, particularly Larry Schiller, who gathered information during the course of the events he narrates. In addition, his afterword details his sources, methods, and even the material that he says provided a "subtext" for the work by forming his perceptions of the prison life Gilmore had known.) In addition, Capote has admitted selecting his materials according to whether they agreed with his own interpretation. (Mailer orders contradictory views in a narrative of more massive detail.) The result is that, however factual *In Cold Blood* may be, Capote appears to have stretched the material in ways disturbingly close to the approximating illusions associated with realistic fiction, while continuing to claim a journalistic contract. Mailer's book, in contrast, appears to adhere more strictly to journalistic standards of accuracy, while it more frankly admits to the complex role of inevitably fictionalizing consciousness. It seems much more factually credible, fictionally lifelike, and thematically rich (though it, too, will have to stand up to future inquiry in this area).

In *The Armies of the Night, Of a Fire on the Moon,* and *The Executioner's Song,* Mailer has clearly varied his methods and stance concerning his self-perceived relation to his subject. But what has not wavered is his combining of a journalistic contract with devices of metafiction, his frank presentation of fact through the orderings of consciousness. The result has been one of the major literatures of the postmodern era, a literature offering mimetic and interpretive power where realistic fiction and conventional journalism have proven unsatisfactory.

4

Journalism and Parody:
The Bestial Comedies
of Hunter S. Thompson

> I am growing extremely weary of writing constantly about
> politics. My brain has become a steam-vat; my body is turning
> to wax and bad flab; impotence looms; my fingernails are
> growing at a fantastic rate of speed—they are turning into
> claws; my standard-size clippers will no longer cut the growth,
> so now I carry a set of huge toe-nail clippers and sneak off every
> night around dusk, regardless of where I am—in any city, ham-
> let, or plastic hotel room along the campaign trail—to chop
> another quarter of an inch or so off of all ten fingers.
>
> People are beginning to notice, I think, but fuck them. I am
> beginning to notice some of *their* problems, too.
>
> —*Fear and Loathing: On the Campaign Trail '72*

Capote and Mailer established their literary reputations with strong first novels in the late 1940's. Both failed to
satisfy subsequent critical expectations over the next decade,
however; as a result, they moved into journalism in the 1960's
with a combination of fanfare and caution.[1] However much their
reputations might have declined during the 1950's, they had still
enjoyed the considerable literary status of novelists, and the
presentation of their journalistic works in such new guises as
"nonfiction novel" and "history as a novel" was certainly, in
part, a strategy for dealing with the inevitable accusations that
they had descended to writing mere journalism. This caution
affected the forms of their journalistic experiments, which are
essentially conservative and traditional. If the journalistic contracts were removed, readers of a far earlier period could be
reasonably comfortable with *In Cold Blood* and *The Armies of*

the Night, for these works have ample formal precedents in American literature.

In turning to two other new journalists of major rank, Hunter S. Thompson and Tom Wolfe, we move to consider new journalistic works that are much more closely linked, in formal terms, to experiments in contemporary fiction. Both writers are relatively young men who first made their literary reputations in the 1960's as journalists revolting against the conventions of their profession. They developed their new journalistic forms with a nearly anarchic sense of freedom and possibility; unlike the novelists, they could only feel their movement into experimental journalism as a bid to ascend in literary status and achievement. Lacking published novels, they developed their forms and techniques with relatively little regard for critical expectations. Capote and Mailer wrote journalism in the form of the novel; Thompson and Wolfe wrote journalism in forms much more uniquely their own.

The latter writers are even more closely comparable to the fabulators than they are to Capote and Mailer. Thompson and Wolfe have developed techniques similar to those of other writers who first made their reputations in the 1960's—Kurt Vonnegut, Jerzy Kosinski, Thomas Pynchon, Donald Barthelme, Ishmael Reed, Robert Coover. While all four of the new journalists treated in this study create works which combine a journalistic contract with a form that tends toward fable, Thompson and Wolfe move away from the devices of realism almost altogether, writing journalism that reads remarkably like the parodic works of fabulation. This is especially true of Hunter S. Thompson, whom Jerome Klinkowitz has identified as so similar in technique to Vonnegut that he has separated him from the new journalists and classified him as a "SuperFictionist." [2] I have been arguing that the opposite contracts of the new journalist and the fabulator have led them to similar forms. If one compares Thompson's *Fear and Loathing: On the Campaign Trail '72* to such a major fabulation as Vonnegut's *Slaughterhouse-Five,* one finds that these two works define an interface where the two forms meet. Both confront their subjects with the controlling power of parody, bringing an insistent application of acknowledged artifice, comic burlesque, and bizarre fantasy to them. The two authors even play with each other's author-reader contracts, Vonnegut seeding his fabulation with facts and Thompson spicing his journalism with fantasies. In so doing, they bypass realism to create uniquely imaginative works, one of new journalism and the other of fabulation—in this case, labels that become as similar as they are distinct.

Thompson began his career as a sportswriter before moving into free-lance writing for such magazines as *The Reporter* and *The National Observer*. An assignment for *The Nation* eventually led to his writing one of the seminal, if stylistically unremarkable, early works of new journalism, *Hell's Angels: A Strange and Terrible Saga* (1966). He soon developed the form he calls "gonzo journalism," [3] producing a large number of articles and two major works in its manic first-person style, *Fear and Loathing in Las Vegas: A Savage Journey to the Heart of the American Dream* (1971) and *Fear and Loathing: On the Campaign Trail '72* (1973), which have established him as an original (and certainly the most controversial) new journalist. In these works Thompson has developed a journalism which communicates, both formally and thematically, his black humorist vision. The pervasive theme of Thompson's work is one of "doomed alienation on your own turf." [4] In his "fear and loathing" works he has expressed this malaise through an innovative application of the same parodic devices found in black-humor fictions. The result is journalism which reads as savage cartoon.

Thompson achieves the freedom to break with realism by extending the central metafictional device in Mailer's *Armies of the Night*. He presents facts through two versions of the self, narrator and participant personae, who are separated by time and perspective. Since, as implied author, he presents all of the facts in the works as perceptions of one or the other of these personae, Mailer is free to develop the subject matter as his personal construct of actual events. By keeping differences in time and perspective negligible, Thompson creates only one persona who serves as both narrator and protagonist. This persona may appear at first as a simpler creation, a mere self-caricature; but that self-caricature is in fact a highly sophisticated tool, which the actual Hunter Thompson manipulates as calculatingly as Laurence Sterne did Tristram Shandy.

As the shaping authorial mind behind the narrating persona, Thompson creates a self-caricature who is extremely disoriented, both by actual events and by paranoid illusions—often induced by liquor or drugs—present in his own consciousness. Presenting journalistic events through the perceptions of this maddened, even hallucinating, persona, Thompson presents his black humorist vision of those actual events without violating their actuality. Like a mad seer or a holy fool, this persona can reveal aspects of events not readily apparent to those with normal perception. Through self-caricature Thompson is able to take Mailer's metafictional journalism into the more radically fictive world of parody.

Thompson uses the persona as his narrator much as Ken Kesey uses the mad Chief Broom in *One Flew Over the Cuckoo's Nest*. Since he presents his journalism as the disoriented persona's vision and experience of events, Thompson is free to present journalistic material through the licenses of parody. He can flatten and warp his representations of actuality without falsifying them, because he has clearly represented them as products of a flattening and warping mind. Like Chief Broom, the persona is in part a narrative device which can be used to distort the surfaces of realism in order to reveal their underlying truth. Through prose that seems as offhand as it is brilliantly expressionistic (Morris Dickstein has called it "one of the few original prose styles of recent years, a style dependent almost deliriously on insult, vituperation, and steam-of-invective to a degree unparalleled since Céline" [5]), Thompson's persona constructs a work which is simultaneously report and surreal vision, a frightening world populated by predatory animals motivated primarily by instinct and appetite.

Because the persona is so crucial to Thompson's journalism, the traits of this self-caricature should be briefly outlined before we examine the works themselves. As a vehicle of parody, the persona is first of all clearly not what E. M. Forster called a "round" or "realistic" character. He has virtually no complexity of thought or motivation, and he does not undergo subtle changes from experience. He is instead a two-dimensional cartoon character, a caricature resulting from Thompson's "flatten-ing" and exaggeration of certain of his own characteristics. Thompson identifies his persona closely with certain vivid trademark objects and mannerisms as a substitute for the subtle complexities of a realistic characterization; he provides him with a dual nature that embodies the innocent idealism and compulsive violence found also in America's national character; and he portrays him as a trickster figure.

The close identification of the hero (or anti-hero) with trademark objects and mannerisms is a common gimmick of popular narrative, from detective novels to comic books and adventure movies. Ian Fleming, for instance, compensated for James Bond's lack of a round, realistic character by giving him an almost unnatural affinity for certain types of cars, guns, cigarettes, drinks, and female features. Sherlock Holmes is an earlier example, and the heroes of comic books and melodramatic fiction of all sorts have always had certain costumes, weapons, vehicles, and gestures. Joining black-humor fiction writers in sacrificing rounded character for flat effect, Thompson has followed many of them in investing his persona with trademark fetishes: a love for Wild Turkey bourbon, exotic cars, powerful handguns, the Vincent Black Shadow motorcycle, Doberman pinschers, drugs, extremely amplified music, and violent rhetoric. Without these trademarks the persona's character is little more than a flat and predictable (though highly engaging and volatile) mixture of "fear and loathing."

Thompson's self-caricature is a paradox of compulsive violence and outraged innocence, an emblem of the author's schizophrenic view of America. His attachment to handguns and vicious dogs reveals his tendencies toward violence and paranoia, tendencies which are also apparent in his hyperbolic prose style. But the persona also has a determined belief in the power of good intentions and right methods which runs counter to his violent impulses. Despite the psychotic threatening, his artistic aims include the corrective impulse of satire. Observing this aspect of Thompson's persona, Kurt Vonnegut has proposed that such innocence be named after him: "From this moment on, let all those who feel that Americans can be as easily led to beauty as to ugliness, to truth as to public relations, to joy as to bitter-

ness, be said to be suffering from Hunter Thompson's disease." [6]
This identification of one side of the persona's character with the
Emersonian strain in America is further reinforced by his choice
of residence in the isolated wilderness of Colorado. After each
major work Thompson returns to his home in Woody Creek in
order to recover from America's corruption, and in the guise of
his persona he emphasizes this return as a necessary ritual. In
addition to needing the purity of nature, his persona shows
interest in money only as the means to his reckless freedom, and
shares the traditional American hero's reluctance to become
involved with the females whom he encounters on his travels.
While he parodies America's impulses to violence and paranoia,
the persona is untainted by the same society's lusts for conquest
and possession.

The created persona is essentially defined by the title phrase,
"fear and loathing," for it embodies both the paranoia with
which the persona perceives the ominous forces pervading
actuality, and the aggression with which he seeks to survive it.
This latter trait is particularly crucial, for despite the comic
buffoonery and paranoid delusions, Thompson's persona is
hardly a passive anti-hero. A descendant of the trickster character of folklore, the Vice of medieval drama, the picaro of early
prose narratives, he is a self-portrait of the journalist as rogue.
Like his literary ancestors, he is a shape-shifter who uses cunning
and agility to survive the dangers of his environment. As he says
in *Fear and Loathing in Las Vegas*, "We are all wired into a
survival trip now." [7] But as a journalist and a human being
attempting to report contemporary events, the dangers he meets
are psychological and spiritual. Defining himself through
opposition, he counters them with violence and laughter.

For this reason Thompson's persona narrates events with a
comically brutal prose and participates in them with comically
cruel pranks. Like Kosinski's protagonist in *Cockpit*, he must
continually attack in order to resist. Like Vonnegut's narrative
persona, he must laugh in order to remain sane. The anarchic and
warlike sound of "gonzo" is appropriate to Thompson's journalism, for it is, both in the persona's adventures as participant and
in his rhetoric as narrator, an individual rebellion against the
homogenization and perversion of man. Faced with the task of

reporting falsity and horror, he resorts to self-induced hallucination, laughter, vengeance, and invention—all acts of reckless freedom which serve as weapons for survival.

In thus outlining the traits of the persona, I do not mean to imply that the actual Hunter Thompson does not share them. Rather, he has purposely emphasized and exaggerated certain of his traits in order to create a fictive version of himself which is essentially a self-caricature, not an in-depth representation of a complex human being. Nevertheless, a further confusion arises from Thompson's having carried this creation of a persona over into his lectures, interviews, and general public exposure. In addition, caricatures of the caricature have been offered to the public by Gary Trudeau in his "Uncle Duke" of the *Doonesbury* comic strip, and by comedian Bill Murray in his portrayal of Thompson in the lamentable film *Where the Buffalo Roam*. Like so many of the rock stars whom he admires (and with whom he has shared space in *Rolling Stone*), Thompson's most crucial creation is himself. Robert Sam Anson, who researched Thompson's career at *Rolling Stone*, reports the following:

The "crazy" Hunter Thompson—The "Raoul Duke," who, as his official *Rolling Stone* biography had it, "lives with . . . an undetermined number of large dobermans trained to kill, in a fortified retreat somewhere in the mountains of Colorado"—was no more than a cover, an elaborate disguise devised to conceal a warm, generous, rather shy man who wanted nothing so much as to be a writer, and concluded that great writers had to be, by their very nature, a little larger than life.

That Hunter Thompson reverenced writing, the way other men worship a god or a rock star, and he worked at it—hard. Years before, as a clerk for *Time*, Thompson had spent evening after evening laboriously copying pages of Faulkner and Fitzgerald, trying to unravel the genius of their rhythms—"learning," as he put it, "how to build a house from the ground up." Later, he traveled west to California, learning, on the road, because that is what Kerouac had done, and he wanted to be like Kerouac. He worried over his own talent, and joked to his doctor that if he didn't use drugs, he would "have the mind of a second-rate accountant." When it came time to write, he put away most of the drugs and concentrated on his craft, sculpting each sentence and paragraph with a care and precision that belied the stream-of-consciousness Gonzo style.[8]

While faint glimmerings of the persona are apparent in a few passages of *Hell's Angels*, Thompson began developing this character as a complete concept in two articles published in 1970 in the now defunct *Scanlan's Monthly*, "The Temptations of Jean-Claude Killy" and "The Kentucky Derby Is Decadent and Depraved." They are included, along with his early, more conventional work as well as his most recent articles, in the retrospective collection entitled *The Great Shark Hunt* (1979). In *Fear and Loathing in Las Vegas*, however, he first achieved major success. Similar in form to the Derby article, *Fear and Loathing in Las Vegas* is far more effective and complex. Aside from being Thompson's first major literary achievement, it is also a significant curiosity in the parallel development of fabulation and new journalism, for in it Thompson has established a confusion of their opposed contracts. In *Fear and Loathing in Las Vegas* Thompson creates a verbal construct in which the reader is never sure whether he is experiencing extraordinary fact or extraordinary fantasy. He is only sure that it is not realism. Thompson achieves this unique contract through the device of the persona.

One indication of how self-consciously Thompson regards his persona as a character whom he has created for specific purposes is apparent in his giving him two different names. In *Fear and Loathing in Las Vegas* the persona calls himself Raoul Duke, while in *Fear and Loathing: On the Campaign Trail '72* he calls himself Dr. Hunter S. Thompson. In both books the character jokingly refers to the name he is not using as if it signified another person.[9] For purposes of clarity I will use these two names or the term "persona" in discussing the character who appears as narrator and protagonist in these works, and I will use the name "Thompson" when referring to the actual man who exists outside these constructs and as implied author.

Originally appearing in *Rolling Stone* magazine in two installments in 1971, *Fear and Loathing in Las Vegas* is, in barest outline, the author's purported autobiographical confession of his failure to fulfill the magazine's assignment to "cover" two events in Las Vegas, the Fourth Annual "Mint 400" motorcycle desert race and the National Conference of District Attorneys Seminar on Narcotics and Dangerous Drugs. It is more exactly the author's (or "Raoul Duke's") tale of his hallucinations and adventures while with a 300-pound Samoan attorney called Dr. Gonzo, actually a Chicano lawyer named Oscar Zeta Acosta (the identity was changed at the insistence of the publisher's lawyers), who serves as a parody of noble savage "sidekicks" from Chingachgook to Tonto. The book is, then, even in its most general subject and presentation, either a report of an actual experience which was largely fantasy or an actual fantasy which is disguised as report. Journalism only in the loosest sense, what is reported is the state of the persona's mind and, metaphorically, of the nation.

Epistemological and ontological ambiguity is communicated in the opening sentence: "We were somewhere around Barstow on the edge of the desert when the drugs began to take hold" (p. 3). By thus combining observed data with an admittedly altered consciousness, Thompson signals the reader that the narrating persona, Raoul Duke, is taking him on a journey both actual and hallucinatory: "suddenly there was a terrible roar all around us and the sky was full of what looked like huge bats, all swooping and screeching and diving around the car, which was going about a hundred miles an hour with the top down to Las Vegas" (p. 3). The narrator presents two justifications, one formal and one thematic, for his methods. First, he explains that he approached the assignment with a collection of every known mind-expanding drug because he felt that he would have to invent his story: "But what *was* the story? Nobody had bothered to say. So we would have to drum it up on our own. Free Enterprise. The American Dream. Horatio Alger gone mad on drugs in Las Vegas. Do it *now*: pure Gonzo journalism" (p. 12).

With this statement Thompson sets forth the formal aesthetic of the work. Saddled with a reportorial assignment to which he brings no preconceived "fiction" or world-view (in contrast both to the preformed clichés of conventional journalists and to Mailer's elaborate philosophical scheme), he asserts that he will have to turn to the powers of his consciousness to invent meaning. Opening his mind to the interior hallucinations of drugs and the exterior hallucinations of Las Vegas, he will create a fable. But because any such invented meaning will be of questionable value, the fable must be constructed as a self-conscious literary parody complete with capitalized themes (The American Dream) and archetypal characters (Horatio Alger). In content, *Fear and Loathing in Las Vegas* is to be report as invention; in form, account as fable. With this parody of a journalistic aesthetic Thompson becomes, as Jonathan Raban characterized him in his extremely unfavorable review of the book, "a professionally unreliable witness." [10] He uses new journalism to write fabulation, placing his work on an "edge" between fact and fantasy. [11]

Thompson makes his second justification for his methods on a thematic level. Exposing the theme with a distancing irony by calling it "the socio-psychic factor," he nevertheless makes it clear that the parodic quest after the American Dream is also a painfully serious flight from a corrupted condition: "Every now and then when your life gets complicated and the weasels start closing in, the only real cure is to load up on heinous chemicals and then drive like a bastard from Hollywood to Las Vegas. To *relax*, as it were, in the womb of the desert sun" (p. 12). This parody of the American Adam's archetypal desire to escape the complications of civilization is to be also a comment on that quest's contemporary perversion. The protagonist, threatened by the "weasels" (which suggest an active corruption), is traveling east, not west, seeking rebirth not in the solitude of the forest but in the isolation of the desert.

These authorial inversions of the conventional reporter's approach to actuality and the traditional American hero's search for fulfillment result from a single response to the unreality of contemporary America. For Thompson, the landscape of America in the 1970's is itself hallucinatory, and Las Vegas, America's dream city, epitomizes it. Viewing the city through his own countering hallucinations, Thompson's persona sees a world differing from the surrounding desert only in its artificiality, for the impulses of society and nature appear predatory to him. Upon their initial arrival, for instance, Raoul Duke enters the hotel bar with his attorney, to discover the following: "Terrible things were happening all around us. Right next to me a huge reptile was gnawing on a woman's neck, the carpet was a blood-soaked sponge—impossible to walk on it, no footing at all" (p. 24). Later Duke flees Las Vegas and rushes into the desert, only to find himself shooting at gila monsters which he suspects are stalking him (p. 99). In either setting, city or desert, society or nature, the persona's drugged perceptions reveal the same underlying reality: a world reptilian in its ferocity.

Duke's drugged perceptions also expose the ominous distortion of the landscape produced by the Las Vegas architecture. When he and Gonzo escape the predatory scene in the bar by retreating to their room, the chemical hallucinations have lessened to the point where he is no longer "seeing huge pterodactyls lumbering around the corridors in pools of fresh blood" (p. 27). Nevertheless, he now finds that the environment itself seems predatory, with the view from his window affording visions as disturbing as those induced by drugs. Watching a gigantic neon sign which makes a loud hum as it blocks the natural view of the mountains, he gasps, "There's a big . . . machine in the sky, . . . some kind of electric snake . . . coming straight at us" (p. 27). Through his persona's hallucinating perceptions, Thompson is able to present Las Vegas's psychic dangers as physical ones.

When Duke and Gonzo leave the room, they go to the Circus-Circus casino. Here people gamble while costumed performers provide continuing spectacles on nets suspended high above the tables. Thompson's persona describes the effect of looking up while gambling, only to see "a half-naked fourteen-year-old girl being chased through the air by a snarling wolverine, which is suddenly locked in a death battle with two silver-painted Polacks who come swinging down from opposite balconies and meet in mid-air on the wolverine's neck" (p. 46). Customers on the upstairs balconies are shooting "the pasties off the nipples of a ten-foot bulldyke" in order to "win a cotton-candy goat" (p. 47), while others pay "just 99¢" to have their likenesses appear on a two-hundred-foot-tall screen in downtown Las Vegas.

Such sights convince Duke that drugs are particularly dangerous in Las Vegas, because "reality itself is too twisted" (p. 47). *Fear and Loathing in Las Vegas* continues to alternate between and merge such interior and exterior hallucinations. As a result, the reader is made aware of how artificial, distorted, and finally unreal the neon actuality of contemporary America is. The primary difference between the hallucinatory visions that afflict Duke and his attorney, and the hallucinating actuality that they find in the landscape of Las Vegas, is that the former originate within the self and are thus potentially controllable. In addition, they counter the general unreality by putting its ominous qualities in sharper perspective. The persona's drug-visions thus afford a truth similar to that which we associate with the visions of a mad seer.

But while drugs have advantages as weapons of survival (Dr. Gonzo refers to taking them as being "armed"), Duke and Gonzo employ laughter as their most necessary defense. Many critics of black-humorist fictions have commented on comedy's ability to distance one from horror, to allow some degree of psychic control and thus survival. Duke protects himself from both his own and others' horrors through unrelenting humor. When he has trouble walking on the "blood-soaked sponge" of barroom carpet, for instance, he immediately attempts to transform his terror into a joke: " 'Order some golf shoes,' I whispered. 'Otherwise, we'll never get out of this place alive. You notice these lizards don't have any trouble moving around in this muck—that's because they have *claws* on their feet.' " (p. 24). Soon after, when he views the neon sign as a gigantic snake, he responds to Gonzo's advice to "shoot it" with a dead-pan reply: " 'Not yet,' I said. 'I want to study its habits' " (p. 27). The ability to laugh at horrors that are really only hallucinations, whether personal or societal, enables the psyche to survive in a world which seems predatory and savage.

There is, however, an actuality beyond the hallucinations of drugs and Las Vegas, a world which is so real that laughter cannot serve as an effective weapon against it. Years ago Burton Feldman attacked black humor as inadequate in the face of "Auschwitz, or King Leopold in the Congo, or Hiroshima," and asserted that "a reader can only be agreed with if he concludes that the world is surely worse than Black Humor is telling him." [12] But Charles Harris has pointed out that in black humorist works "realistic incidents frequently intrude upon the fantastic and grotesque" in a way that "results in reader disorientation." [13]

Thompson gains precisely this effect by interspersing Duke's hallucinatory and comic experience in Las Vegas with various all-too-actual experiences brought in from the outside world by the media. These "objective" reports present *actual* nightmares; they impinge upon the characters' consciousness with a pressure which compels them to escape into only *apparent* nightmares. In the hotel room, for instance, they briefly turn on the television, only to find a scene more disturbing than the imagined reptiles they have just left: "The TV news was about the Laos Invasion— a series of horrifying disasters: explosions and twisted wreckage, men fleeing in terror, Pentagon generals babbling insane lies. 'Turn that shit off!' screamed my attorney. 'Let's get *out* of here!' " (p. 29). But escape into their automobile only brings "The Battle Hymn of Lieutenant Calley" from the radio, causing Duke to think, "No! I *can't* be hearing this! It must be the drug" (p. 32). Later Duke confronts headlines about a dead girl found stuffed into a refrigerator, official involvement in the heroin traffic in Vietnam, American torture of Vietnamese prisoners, meaningless sniper killings in New York, and a pharmacy owner's selling of dangerous drugs (pp. 72-74). Thompson includes some of these stories in paragraph-length excerpts, so that their "objective" prose stands in counterpoint to the book's agitated style. As a result, the reader himself returns to the hallucinatory and comic narrative with the same relief that the persona feels when he returns to the hallucinations and comic adventures. The parodic invention which is this "report" becomes itself both defense and escape for the reader.

In a number of episodes in *Fear and Loathing in Las Vegas* Duke and Gonzo play cruel (albeit largely rhetorical) pranks upon other characters. These scenes may appear to be the worst kind of smug ridicule directed against the ordinary and unsuspecting; certainly they would be of questionable taste if Thompson's persona did not portray himself as such a paranoid madman. But, as Tom Wolfe has pointed out, "Thompson, for all his surface ferocity, usually casts himself as a frantic loser, inept and half-psychotic, somewhat after the manner of Céline." [14] Moreover, these scenes do not show contempt for particular individuals so much as they reveal the fears and appetites which make people capable of tolerating, or even of perpetrating, barbarism. The pranks are thus partly satirical in their motivation.

One example is Thompson's portrayal of the gulling of a

Georgia district attorney by Duke and Gonzo as they pose as district attorneys from California. Playing upon the district attorney's knowledge of the Manson case, they tell him that cults of Satan worshipers, composed of drug addicts and Vietnam veterans, have been killing people for their blood:

> "Naw!" he said. "That's science fiction stuff!"
>
> "Not where *we* operate," said my attorney. "Hell, in Malibu alone, these goddamn Satan-worshippers kill six or eight people *every day*." He paused to sip his drink. "And all they want is the blood," he continued. "They'll take people right off the street if they have to." He nodded. "Hell, yes. Just the other day we had a case where they grabbed a girl right out of a McDonald's hamburger stand. She was a waitress. About sixteen years old . . . with a lot of people watching, too!"
>
> "What happened?" said our friend. "What did they *do* to her?" He seemed very agitated by what he was hearing.
>
> "*Do?*" said my attorney. "Jesus Christ man. They chopped her goddamn head off right there in the parking lot! Then they cut all kinds of holes in her and sucked out the blood!"
>
> "God *almighty!*" The Georgia man exclaimed . . . "and nobody *did* anything?" [pp. 146-47]

Duke assures the district attorney that they are handling the problem secretly, by forming death squads which use Doberman pinschers to cripple the Satanists before cutting off their heads. The district attorney's response to their advice not to tell the press is to exclaim, "Hell no! . . . We'd never hear the goddamn end of it" (p. 149). His eager acceptance of the reality of the most exaggerated tales of horror Duke and Gonzo can invent, as well as his equally easy acceptance of virtually identical counter-measures, suggests the extent of paranoia and hatred across America.[15] Through such pranks Thompson's persona, functioning as a trickster, reveals that "fear and loathing" are a national affliction, even as he gains some distance from them through manipulation and ridicule. With a savage glee, he leaves the district attorney, a victim duped by his own easy accession to his worst impulses:

> We left him at the bar, swirling the ice in his drink and not smiling. He was worried about whether or not to tell his wife about it. "She'd never understand," he muttered. "You know how women are."
>
> I nodded. My attorney was already gone, scurrying through a maze

of slot machines toward the front door. I said goodbye to our friend, warning him not to say anything about what we'd told him. [p. 149]

But Thompson's persona does not wish to be savage merely in order to seek vengeance and expose baseness. The primary motivating force is the same one behind the drug-taking and laughter: survival. In a world motivated by appetite, questions of morality and fulfillment become irrelevant, even dangerous: "This place is like the Army: the shark ethic prevails—eat the wounded. In a closed society where everybody's guilty, the only crime is getting caught. In a world of thieves, the only final sin is stupidity" (p. 72). This perception explains Thompson's epigraph for the book: "He who makes a beast of himself gets rid of the pain of being a man." As Raney Stanford has observed in an article on the descendant of the trickster figure in our contemporary literature, "as society increases its power of organizing, controlling, but essentially dehumanizing man's life, man as cunning rat, the shape-shifting demon comes back to prominence in our fiction." [16] The persona must become a beast in order to possess the primitive skills that can insure his survival.

Isolated in a tavern in the middle of the desert, Duke makes this transformation by undergoing a reversal of the traditional Christian revelation and conversion. Abandoning the luxuries of morality and guilt, he tells God, "The final incredible truth is that I am not guilty. All I did was take your gibberish *seriously* . . . and you see where it got me? My primitive Christian instincts have made me a criminal" (p. 87). Casting himself as a monster who can hope to turn fear back upon the world, he warns God (whom he perceives as an indifferent "Great Scorer" and "Great Magnet") that "you'd better take care of me, Lord . . . because if you don't you're going to have me *on your hands*" (p. 87).

This demonic moment is the climax of the work. Up until this point Duke and Gonzo have been moving in a state of absolute fear. Duke himself, deciding that "my margin had sunk to nothing" (p. 78), has ignored his new assignment to cover the District Attorneys' seminar, choosing instead to sneak out of Las Vegas in total paranoia. But from this moment on he counters despair not with paranoia, but with ferocity. Exchanging his "fear" for "loathing," he becomes an aggressive character whose new approach to the dangers of the external world is demonstrated in the parable-like scene which immediately follows. Pursued by a highway policeman, Duke successfully handles the threat through aggression:

Your normal speeder will panic and immediately pull over to the side when he sees the big red light behind him . . . and then he will start apologizing, begging for mercy.

This is wrong. It arouses contempt in the cop-heart. The thing to do—when you're running along about a hundred or so and you suddenly find a red-flashing CHP-tracker on your trail—what you want to do then is *accelerate*. Never pull over with the first siren-howl. Mash it down and make the bastard chase you at speeds up to 120 all the way to the next exit. He will follow. But he won't know what to make of your blinker-signal that says you're about to turn right.

This is to let him know you're looking for a proper place to pull off and talk . . . keep signaling and hope for an off-ramp, one of those uphill side-loops with a sign saying "Max Speed 25" . . . and the trick, at this point, is to suddenly leave the freeway and take him into the chute at no less than a hundred miles an hour.

He will lock his brakes about the same time you lock yours, but it will take him a moment to realize that he's about to make a 180-degree turn at this speed . . . but you will be *ready* for it, braced for the Gs and the fast heel-toe work, and with any luck at all you will have come to a complete stop off the road at the top of the turn and be standing beside your automobile by the time he catches up.

He will not be reasonable at first . . . but no matter. Let him calm down. He will want the first word. Let him have it. His brain will be in turmoil: he may begin jabbering, or even pull his gun. Let him unwind; keep smiling. The idea is to show him that you were always in total control of yourself and your vehicle—while *he* lost control of everything. [pp. 90-91]

The key words are "but you will be *ready* for it." It is with this aesthetic of aggression (the same one which informs the book's style) that Duke returns to Las Vegas to "infiltrate" the drug conference. *Fear and Loathing in Las Vegas* turns from a dominant ethos of paranoia in Part I to one of revenge in Part II.

Thompson presents these various aspects of *Fear and Loathing in Las Vegas*—the drug-induced hallucinations of the two main characters, the hallucinatory landscape of Las Vegas, the horrors brought in through the news media, the defensive laughter, the predatory vision of the society, the self-transformation of the protagonist into a beast in order to survive—within a structural pattern based on a self-conscious parody of the quest for the American Dream. This motif is provided not simply through the subtle patterning of the implied author, but as the joking concept of the characters themselves, Duke and Gonzo. Duke says that this is to be a contemporary tale of the great American historical-mythical-literary archetypes: "Free Enterprise. The American Dream. Horatio Alger gone mad on drugs in Las Vegas" (p. 12). The self-consciousness of the persona in making this quest is important, for it reduces the American Dream to parody. Because disillusionment with America's ideals, the exposure of American values as self-deceptions, has so long been typical of modern American literature (*An American Tragedy, The Great Gatsby*), the search for those ideals can no longer be undertaken seriously. The American Dream has so long been isolated and exposed that the contemporary writer, however keenly he feels it as both need and loss, can treat it only as a joke.

As a result, the persona and his companion view their character traits as self-conscious caricatures of the clichés of Free Enterprise and Horatio Alger, pursuing their quest for the American Dream in terms of a melodramatic spy mission. In one scene Gonzo is watching *Mission Impossible* on the hotel television (p. 130); this show, as well as other suspense melodramas, provides the two main characters with a structure through which they can playfully control the paranoia and aggression which otherwise dominate their quest. Duke's account of how the quest was set in motion by *Rolling Stone*'s phoned assignment to cover the Mint 400 begins this motif:

The Dwark approached our table cautiously, as I recall, and when he handed me the pink telephone I said nothing, merely listened. And then I hung up, turning to face my attorney. "That was headquarters," I said. "They want me to go to Las Vegas at once, and make contact with a Portuguese photographer named Lacerda. He'll have the details. All I have to do is check into my suite and he'll seek me out."

My attorney said nothing for a moment, then he suddenly came alive in his chair. "God *hell*!" he exclaimed. "I think I see the *pattern*. This one sounds like real trouble!" [p. 8]

Duke and Gonzo return to this private parody of a spy mission periodically, particularly at moments of decision or extreme pressure. Even as characters moving within the narrative, they contrive a stylized vision which enables them to distance themselves from experience as they confront it. It is easier to play at seeking a literary grail called the American Dream, than it is to live without such irony in the society which perpetrates these illusions. By playing at these pursuits, they avoid the self-deception of the masses in that society. Play in life, like parody in fiction, has the advantage of never taking its actions seriously.

Beyond this spy-melodrama motif, the quest develops in a number of other ways which parody and comment upon the archetype and the impulses behind it. The book opens with the characters speeding east, toward a city in the desert. This inversion of the historical movement toward the west suggests the confused desperation of a frontierless contemporary America. In addition, the drug-taking and the exploitative abandon with which they use the magazine's expense account parody Free Enterprise and Horatio Alger. "Do it *now*" (p. 12) expresses the philosophy of Gonzo journalism, and of American acquisitiveness.

The climactic pattern of the book is a parody of escape and return, the pattern which R. W. B. Lewis has shown in *The American Adam* to be basic to classic American romances. Early in the narrative Duke and Gonzo believe they have found the "vortex" of the American Dream in the gambling and perverse spectacle of the Circus-Circus casino:

"I hate to say this," said my attorney as we sat down at the Merry-Go-Round Bar on the second balcony, "but this place is getting *to* me. I think I'm getting the Fear."

"Nonsense," I said. "We came out here to find the American Dream, and now that we're right in the vortex you want to quit." I grabbed his bicep and squeezed. "You must *realize*," I said, "that we've found the main nerve."

"I know," he said. "That's what gives me the Fear." [pp. 47-48]

This realization, exacerbated (or, perhaps, more clearly revealed) by drugs, induces a state of paranoia that soon causes Duke to sneak out of the hotel and race into the desert, taking with him,

for a reason he cannot determine, "six hundred bars of translu-
cent Neutrogena soap" which he and Gonzo had acquired while
in their room (p. 70). His flight with this "treasure" parodies the
great American tales of doomed journeys with illicit riches, from
McTeague to *Easy Rider*. But Duke eventually decides that he
must return to face the nightmare world he has tried to escape.

But before returning he dismisses feelings of guilt and, in the
scene in the desert described earlier, transforms himself into a
demonic character, an aggressive trickster capable of dealing
with society on its own terms. After ridiculing and exploiting the
district attorneys' drug seminar, Duke and Gonzo enter their
newly rented white Cadillac convertible (called the Whale, in an
obvious parody of the *Moby-Dick* quest) and resume their search
for the American Dream. A waitress and cook, mistaking their
questions in a scene which burlesques the significance of the
search for literary abstractions, give them directions to a club
called The American Dream on Paradise Boulevard. When Duke
and Gonzo arrive at the spot, they find only "a huge slab of
cracked, scorched concrete in a vacant lot full of tall weeds" and
learn that the club "had burned down about three years ago"
(p. 168).

Their quest seemingly over, Duke completes the pattern of
return by returning alone to the Circus-Circus, where he and
Gonzo had earlier feared that they really had found the American
Dream. He intends to purchase an ape that he had seen amid the
Casino's spectacles: "Psychedelics are almost irrelevant in a
town where you can wander into a casino any time of the day or
night and witness the crucifixion of a gorilla—on a flaming neon
cross that suddenly turns into a pinwheel, spinning the beast
around in wild circles above the crowded gambling action"
(p. 190). The ape on the spinning neon cross serves as a parody of
natural man in contemporary American society. The persona's
desire to release the ape from his neon cross and to take him to his
own home in the Colorado mountains, on a plane in which "I've
already reserved two first-class seats—R. Duke and Son"
(p. 190), is a gesture as moving as it is absurd. His Christian
values momentarily reasserting themselves, Duke recognizes his
"Son" as a natural creature and victim, a mirror-image of the
beast he has made himself into, whom he must liberate from

society's corruption. He demands that the owner sell the ape to him, but finally relents when he decides that the sale would only lead to their arrest: "It would take [the ape] a while to calm down, after the shock of being put behind bars, and I couldn't afford to wait around" (p. 191).

Once again, faced with the need to survive, the persona has repressed his Christian impulses. When at last he lands in Denver and sees the Rocky Mountains, he repeats the question he asked so often during his adventures in Las Vegas: "What the fuck was I doing *here?*" (p. 203). His quest has taught him nothing about his direction, about the meaning of the American Dream. But, alone in a land which has become unnatural and savage in the pursuit of that Dream, he has at least learned how to survive. He ends the book with a parodic, and therefore ironic, assertion of that power: "I felt like a monster reincarnation of Horatio Alger . . . a Man on the Move, and just sick enough to be totally confident" (p. 204).

In *Fear and Loathing in Las Vegas* Thompson bypassed the conventions of traditional journalism and realistic fiction to create a work which confused the author-reader contracts of new journalism and of fabulation. Quite aware of the trick he had brought off, he professed to be unsure any longer of what parts had actually happened and what parts were imaginary.[17] As an account of his experience of the Las Vegas assignment, the distinction was probably irrelevant. He confronted the problem of reporting a "story" he didn't understand by inventing one of his own, and the result is an important report on the American unreality of the late 1960's. Lurking behind that report, making their presences known to the characters through the media at various key points in the narrative, are the Vietnam war and the President who claimed to be ending it even as he widened it. At one point Raoul Duke bitterly expresses the alienation of living "here in 'our own country'—in this doomstruck era of Nixon" (p. 178). Two years later, Thompson set out to chronicle the attempt to remove Richard Nixon from the White House and to end the war.

For one full year he followed the presidential campaign. His monthly reports to *Rolling Stone* became the required reading of other reporters covering the election,[18] and gained a new prestige both for Thompson and for the counterculture magazine. After the campaign they were issued as *Fear and Loathing: On the Campaign Trail '72*. The collection of monthly and biweekly reports forms a public journal of his adventures and opinions as he followed the events and personalities of the campaign. While an introduction and epitaph, occasional footnotes, and a few interpolated passages contribute to overall continuity, the book is loosely episodic. Despite the apparent spontaneity of its composition and the obvious problems inherent in patterning a book which depends on events whose outcomes are unknown even as the chapters are being originally published, the work does have a form—one conferred by the interplay between the course of actual events and the emotional reactions and imaginative orderings of Dr. Hunter S. Thompson, the National Affairs Editor of *Rolling Stone*.

In contrast to the persona in *Las Vegas* (Dr. Thompson jokingly refers to Raoul Duke at various points as an "objective" journalist and the inventor of the Xerox telecopier), Dr. Thompson is a somewhat more restrained figure. In order to cover the important factual material of the presidential campaign, he generally eschews hallucinatory drugs, instead favoring those which merely exaggerate actuality (amphetamines, marijuana, alcohol). Thompson writes of the campaign with an expressionistic license, while nevertheless enjoying a much more journalistic contract with the reader than he made in *Fear and Loathing in Las Vegas*.[19] But his more crucial innovation in this regard is his shifting of the reader's focus from the events of the narrative to the words of the narration. In his review of *Campaign Trail*, Joseph Kanon praised Thompson for being "the kind of writer who talks to you right on the page."[20] By drawing attention to the work's ontological status as an alternatingly disoriented and lucid consciousness's verbal construction on a page, Thompson achieves the freedom to write journalism which meshes report with parody, burlesque, and even fantasy.

Thompson thus takes journalism into the self-reflexive world of metafiction, even farther than did Mailer in *Of a Fire on the Moon*. Like Mailer, Thompson's narrative persona in *Campaign Trail* openly discusses his methods and problems of composition.

And like Mailer, he also presents actual events through a highly mannered and rhetorical prose style. But Thompson goes further than Mailer in keeping a nearly constant focus upon his narrator's consciousness; he never lets the reader forget that he is sitting at a desk in a definite place, composing the account while fully aware of the conditions under which he writes. *Campaign Trail* is the ultimate example of journalism as metafiction, for Thompson constructs the narrative as a mock-melodrama of a chaotic mind's attempt to create an ordered account of chaotic events. In his narration Dr. Thompson, struggling heroically (if only half-successfully) against pressures from within and without, repeatedly falls into digression and fantasy before suddenly regaining control of himself and the subject—only to fall into digression and fantasy once again.

Dr. Thompson's saga is thus an episodic series of a disordered mind's musings, distractions, paranoia, ragings, and occasionally lucid reports. But *Campaign Trail* is actually neither formless nor spontaneous in its structure. Like *Tristram Shandy*, it is the highly contrived construct of a calculating implied author who communicates experience as a perceived chaos, a chaos tenuously controlled by a consciousness' assertion of meaning upon a page. The overall picaresque structure, subsuming a mixture of reporting, meditation, and digression, represents a mirror-image of the disordered but determined consciousness of Dr. Thompson splicing together his imaginative experience.

Early in the narrative, Dr. Thompson explicitly rejects the illusory orderings of conventional journalism, pretending to forget one of its "Five W's" and saying that the closest thing to "Objective Journalism" he has seen is a "closed-circuit TV setup that watched shoplifters in the General Store at Woody Creek." That video observer was generally ignored unless a known shoplifter appeared: "when that happened, everybody got so excited that the thief had to do something quick, like buy a green popsicle or a can of Coors and get out of the place immediately" (p. 48). Through such parody, Thompson shows how Heisenberg's Indeterminacy Principle is a factor in even the most objective observations. Instead of relying on such illusory empiricism, his reporting attempts to order a reality imaginatively. He overcomes various forces which he parodies in terms of imminent apocalypse: the chaos of actual events, of the pressure of his task, even of his own psychic disorientation. For instance, he precedes his report on the Ohio primary with a portrait of himself forced to sit at his desk in a maelstrom of confusion and pressure:

The phone is ringing again and I can hear Crouse downstairs trying to put them off.

"What the hell are you guys worried about? He's up there cranking out a page every three minutes . . . What? . . . No, it won't make much sense, but I guarantee you we'll have plenty of words. If all else fails we'll start sending press releases and shit like that . . . Sure, why worry? We'll start sending almost immediately."

Only a lunatic would do this kind of work: twenty-three primaries in five months; stone drunk from dawn till dusk and huge speed-blisters all over my head. Where is the meaning? That light at the end of the tunnel?

Crouse is yelling again. They want more copy. He has sent them all of his stuff on the Wallace shooting, and now they want mine. Those halfwit sons of bitches should subscribe to a wire service; get one of those big AP tickers that spits out fifty words a minute, twenty-four hours a day . . . a whole grab-bag of weird news; just rip it off the top and print whatever comes up. Just the other day the AP wire had a story about a man from Arkansas who entered some kind of contest and won a two-week vacation—all expenses paid—wherever he wanted to go. Any place in the world: Mongolia, Easter Island, the Turkish Riviera . . . but his choice was Salt Lake City, and that's where he went.

Is this man a registered voter? Has he come to grips with the issues? Has he bathed in the blood of the lamb?

So much for all that. The noise-level downstairs tells me Crouse will not be able to put them off much longer. So now we will start getting serious: First Columbus, Ohio, and then Omaha. But mainly Columbus, only because this thing began—in *my* head, at least—as a fairly straight and serious account of the Ohio primary. [pp. 186–87]

Wayne Booth has characterized such passages in *Campaign Trail* as gratuitous entertainment: "far too much . . . consists of dodgy waffling precisely like the freshman essay every writing teacher receives at least once a year: 'Sitting in front of my blank page at 2:30 a.m., with the paper due tomorrow, I am desperate. But I have an idea. I'll write about how it feels to be sitting in front of my blank page. . . .' " [21] Yet such passages in Thompson's work function as sophisticated metafictional strategies emphasizing the status of the work as personal construct, and thus shifting its drama from the events reported to that of an individual consciousness's experience of those events. By making Dr. Thompson's writing desk the central fact of his narrative, Thompson is able to present the presidential campaign as an unfolding experience both exterior and interior to Dr. Thompson's consciousness, a process which lacks any apparent objective order and must instead be imaginatively ordered by the perceiving consciousness. Time in Dr. Thompson's narrative is not historical, but spatial.

A historian or realistic novelist, looking at events from a perspective above and outside, perceives a certain cause-and-effect sequence, and then constructs a patterned narrative which creates a seemingly objective order. To bolster this construct as the empirical representation of an actual pattern of events, he endeavors to focus the reader's attention upon the events of the narrative and to make him forget about the artificer who imposes that pattern. By drawing attention to his use of such narrative conventions, Mailer has sought, in *The Armies of the Night* and his other journalism, to make the reader aware of his artificial role while nevertheless carrying it out. In this way he confers the conventional order of the novelist and historian without falsely suggesting that it is objective. But Thompson, by focusing upon his narrator's temporal and physical proximity to the events, makes those events far more formidable and his own ordering powers correspondingly weaker.

The page and deadline become the life and death of Thompson's narrative. The deadline makes the process of composition an act meaningful in itself, for without words there will be nothing—no story. The page on the writing desk becomes the problematic reality that results from the meeting of consciousness and world, the place where Dr. Thompson must overcome the chaos of his subject (and of his mind) in order to contrive something which will fill the blankness. By having Dr. Thompson constantly draw attention to himself in this act of pressured creation, as he seemingly composes through free association, digression, and fantasy, Thompson violates the reader's expectations for a narrative which will mirror an objective pattern of external events. Instead, the "report" mirrors Dr. Thompson's struggle for meaning. Indeed, the passage quoted above—far from being mere entertainment—affords a comically veiled critique of the journalistic "truth" offered by the corporate press under its business pressures, as well as providing a frank evaluation of the provincial vision of the American voter.

By further presenting such "reports" as the construct of a disordered consciousness, Thompson acquires the license to portray the campaign in the distancing and symbolic forms of parody. He has Dr. Thompson begin his chapter on the climactic California primary with a seemingly formless agitation, reporting on his own bestial tendencies and use of the Black Vincent motorcycle. But Thompson, the implied author behind the persona's apparent ravings, is actually preparing the reader for his view of the primary as "one of the most brutal and degrading animal acts of our time" (p. 220). This purpose becomes clear when Dr. Thompson berates himself for again failing to write a conventionally coherent introduction:

> Jesus! Another tangent, and right up front, this time—the whole *lead*, in fact, completely fucked.
> What can I say? Last week I blew the whole thing. Total failure. Missed the deadline, no article, no wisdom, no excuse. . . . Except one: Yes, I was savagely and expertly duped by one of the oldest con trips in politics. [p. 221]

This leads to a self-extending chain of further digressions: a fantasized revenge upon McGovern's evasive campaign manager, Frank Mankiewicz, by severing his big toes; the attempt of a typewriter-rental service to bill Dr. Thompson unfairly; his problems trying to ride an excessively powered motorcycle; his grudge against Democratic chairman Larry O'Brien for supposedly breaking a long-standing promise to award him the governorship of American Samoa. These entertaining but seemingly gratuitous tales lead not to irrelevance, but to a report on the acrimonious character of the political campaign in California.

Similarly, Thompson has Dr. Thompson begin his report on the Old Guard's last-minute maneuverings to prevent McGovern's nomination with a hilarious tall-tale: The night a watchman at Random House, using a metal vacuum-cleaner tube, supposedly beats Dr. Thompson's harmless Blue Indigo snake to death. It had escaped from a cardboard box, causing the watchman to suddenly find himself "menaced by a hissing, six-foot serpent coming fast up the stairs at him from the general direction of Cardinal Spellman's quarters just across the court-yard" (p. 253). This absurdist parable of "fear and loathing" suggests Thompson's interpretation of the forces behind the Stop McGovern movement. Storytelling is made to function as report-ing—reporting that is certainly fabulous, but not in the sense of falsehood.

Thompson uses this "digressive" freedom afforded by dis-ordered consciousness in a number of other ways. He has his persona wander off into fantasies which project his suspicions into concrete images. Thus Dr. Thompson's realization that Mankiewicz manipulates the press for McGovern leads to a paranoid delusion that the campaign manager has physically ambushed him (pp. 362–63). Likewise, Thompson uses the license provided by Dr. Thompson's narrating mind in order to convey a tone of immediacy; the report seems to have been written even as the events were observed. Halfway through the "May" report, Dr. Thompson informs the reader that the rest of the chapter is the result of "about fifty pages of scribbled notes" taken from his notebook and sent "straight to the typesetter" (p. 187). These "notes" provide a minute-by-minute account of the McGovern campaign managers' reactions to the Ohio pri-mary returns as they are transmitted by television and telephone to a Columbus motel room, thus affording a vivid view of the election-night experience for the major participants (pp. 188–201).

Like Mailer, Thompson presents the product of his persona's engagement with actual events through undisguised verbal com-parisons that link observation to perception. Both writers clearly display the ontological status of the style as a combination of fact and mind. But whereas Mailer's narrative persona creates metaphors that are usually subtle, complexly extended, and at times so surprisingly appropriate that they seem to become part of the object's reality, Dr. Thompson appends similes that are blatant, succinct, and so consistently bestial that they reduce the political world of supposedly complex passions and subtle strategies to his own private allegory of appetite.

The nervous rhythms, shifting focus, hyperbolic imagery, extreme presentness, and yet parodic control of this verbal instrument is Thompson's major literary innovation. These traits are all established in the opening paragraph of his introduction to *Campaign Trail*:

Dawn is coming up in San Francisco now: 6:09 A.M. I can hear the rumble of early morning buses under my window at the Seal Rock Inn . . . out here at the far end of Geary Street: this is the end of the line, for buses and everything else, the western edge of America. From my desk I can see the dark jagged hump of "Seal Rock" looming out of the ocean in the grey morning light. About two hundred seals have been barking out there most of the night. Staying in this place with the windows open is like living next to a dog pound. Last night we had a huge paranoid poodle up here in the room, and the dumb bastard went totally out of control when the seals started barking—racing around the room like a chicken hearing a pack of wolves outside the window, howling and whining, leaping up on the bed and scattering my book-galley pages all over the floor, knocking the phone off the hook, upsetting the gin bottles, trashing my carefully organized stacks of campaign photographs . . . off to the right of this typewriter, on the floor between the beds, I can see an 8×10 print of Frank Mankiewicz yelling into a telephone at the Democratic Convention in Miami; but that one will never be used, because the goddamn hound put five big claw-holes in the middle of Frank's chest. [p. 15]

This style conveys the world external to the narrating consciousness as a *perceived* chaos. The irrationality and ferocity of the above scene exist almost completely in the language; even static, inanimate objects are "looming," and a marred photograph displays "five big claw-holes" in a human chest.

The result is a bestial world in which established figures of the Democratic party are on the same page "a gang of senile leeches" and a "herd of venal pigs" (p. 125); a world in which trying to get "anything but pompous bullshit and gibberish" out of one of McGovern's campaign managers is "like trying to steal meat from a hammerhead shark" (p. 234); in which representatives of the media pursue a candidate "like a swarm of wild bees" (p. 237); in which the prospect of Sammy Davis, Jr., ever abandoning a fallen Nixon would be "like a suckfish cutting loose from a mortally wounded shark" (p. 391); in which the nomination of Muskie to oppose Nixon "would have been like sending a three-toed sloth out to seize turf from a wolverine" (p. 159). When Dr. Thompson says that "Hubert Humphrey is the purest and most disgusting example of a Political Animal in American politics today" (p. 205), that media label takes on a whole new coloration.

Within this menagerie, only three figures are set apart. McGovern, whom Dr. Thompson sees as the best of this world, comes "wheeling out of New Hampshire like the Abominable Snowman on a speed trip" (p. 406). The only politician whom Dr. Thompson finds more impressive in person than on television (p. 128), McGovern is seen not as a man who is really a beast, but as a mysterious beast who may really be a kind of man. For Dr. Thompson, this places him well above the typical presidential aspirant. However much he may doubt the reality of McGovern's difference from other politicians as the campaign progresses, by election eve he is sure that the alternative figures of McGovern and Nixon afford a crucial symbolic and psychological choice: "it would be hard to find any two better models in the national politics arena for the legendary *duality*—the congenital Split Personality and polarized instincts—that almost everybody except Americans has long since taken for granted as the key to our National Character" (p. 416). Nixon, Dr. Thompson asserts, "represents that dark, venal, and incurably violent side of the American character almost every other country in the world has learned to fear and despise" (p. 416).

Within the flattened, black-and-white world of Dr. Thompson's consciousness, McGovern and Nixon function as allegorical figures of a struggle for America's soul. Although Nixon is a distant spectre in *Campaign Trail* (Thompson was refused press credentials by the White House), he nevertheless serves as Dr. Thompson's chief antagonist in his quest for a good America. Nixon, in the persona's consciousness, is "America's answer to the monstrous Mr. Hyde":

He speaks for the Werewolf in us; the bully, the predatory shyster who turns into something unspeakable, full of claws and bleeding string-warts, on nights when the moon comes too close. . . .

At the stroke of midnight in Washington, a drooling red-eyed beast with the legs of a man and a head of a giant hyena crawls out of its bedroom window in the South Wing of the White House and leaps fifty feet down to the lawn . . . pauses briefly to strangle the Chow watchdog, then races off into the darkness . . . towards the Watergate, snarling with lust, loping through the alleys behind Pennsylvania Avenue, and trying desperately to remember which one of those four hundred identical balconies is the one outside Martha Mitchell's apartment. . . . [p. 417]

Dr. Thompson's America is a promise betrayed, a possibility of noble humanity which repeatedly reveals itself as only a sick beast. Nixon is hateful because he gives vent to that tendency, a monster whose imminent landslide reelection will assert once and for all the bestiality of the country: "This may be the year when we finally come face to face with ourselves; finally just lay back and say it—that we are really just a nation of 220 million used car salesmen with all the money we need to buy guns, and no qualms at all about killing anybody else in the world who tries to make us uncomfortable" (pp. 413-14). Dr. Thompson's suspicion that this is our true condition is symbolized and parodied at various points through the depiction of his paranoid belief that his own body and mind are regressing into the bestial. As early as the February chapter he describes himself driving "like a werewolf" and wondering if he is "seriously bent" (p. 65) in his desire to pursue the campaign trail; by June he is reporting that he feels himself decaying, and that his fingernails are turning into claws. Throughout the book he provides ominous reports on his own health, until finally he breaks down after the election debacle. At this point, parodying the methods of eighteenth-century fiction, Thompson inserts a supposed "Editor's Note" which informs us that the November chapter has necessarily been completed through a taped interview:

At this point Dr. Thompson suffered a series of nervous seizures in his suite at the Seal Rock Inn. It became obvious both by the bizarre quality of his first-draft work and his extremely disorganized lifestyle that the only way the book could be completed was by means of compulsory verbal composition. Despite repeated warnings from Dr. Thompson's personal physician we determined that for esthetic, historical, and contractual reasons The Work would have to be finished at all costs.

What follows, then, is a transcription of the conversations we had as Dr. Thompson paced around his room—at the end of an eighteen-foot microphone cord—describing the final days of the doomed McGovern campaign. [p. 422]

Thompson portrays disease not only as an interior spiritual condition, but also as a physical corruption of the original promise of America's landscape. Throughout *Campaign Trail* Dr. Thompson perceives the simple rising of the sun as an occurrence placed in doubt by contemporary American society: in Milwaukee in April he reports that "dawn is struggling up through the polluted mist on Lake Michigan to the east" (p. 136); later he sees "a cold grey dawn bloating up out of Lake Michigan" (p. 142). In downtown Los Angeles in June he observes that "dawn comes up on this city like a shitmist" and wonders, "Will the sun eventually poke through?" (p. 222). Another morning in the same month he reports a dawn in which "the sun is fighting through the smog now, a hot grey glow on the street below my window" (p. 244). These reports come during the months when the McGovern campaign is experiencing success, and it seems to Dr. Thompson that the good side of the American character may yet succeed in asserting itself. He describes the dawn of the day after McGovern's nomination as one in which "the sun loomed out of the ocean to light Miami Beach" (p. 378). But then comes the Eagleton disaster, and Dr. Thompson never again reports any dawn in the book. Thompson uses his persona's perceptions of the internal corruption of his own body and the external corruption of the nation's landscape to mirror his perception of America's spiritual perversion.

This concern with the history and future of America is the larger theme of *Campaign Trail*, much more its true concern than the immediate subject of the presidential campaign. Structurally, it is a parodic quest book centered around a symbolic city. The first chapter finds Thompson's persona moving east from his pastoral home in Woody Creek, Colorado, to Washington, D.C., reversing the historical-mythical-literary direction, in order to discover the contemporary reality of a nation that has always moved west in search of a dream. Most of this opening chapter is devoted to Dr. Thompson's discovery of the prevailing state of American alienation. He reports that whites have retreated into an "elegant-looking ghetto," leaving the rest of the city to "black marauders who have turned places like chic Georgetown and once-stylish Capitol Hill into hellishly paranoid Fear Zones" (p. 24). Hearing tales "about coming back to your car and finding the radio aerial torn off, the windshield wipers bent up in the air like spaghetti and all the windows smashed" (p. 24), he discovers that he cannot remain untouched by this atmosphere: "After only ten days in this town I have noticed the Fear Syndrome clouding even my own mind: I find myself ignoring black hitchhikers, and everytime I do it I wonder, 'Why the fuck did you do that?' " (p. 26). In these opening scenes we see the first signs of Dr. Thompson's fear of personal corruption, a fear which eventually develops into a schizophrenic perception of himself as a werewolf.

Despite this feeling of being in the grip of corrupting forces beyond his control or comprehension, a sense of helplessness extending to his perception that as narrator he is "drifting around in the nervous murk of some story with no apparent meaning or spine to it" (p. 242), Dr. Thompson is wonderfully aggressive and humorous, both in his actions and in his rhetoric. He gradually moves from a perspective of skeptical inquiry to one of hope, then to renewed skepticism and ambivalence, and finally to desperate commitment to the McGovern campaign. During this first half of the book he plays pranks and spews abuse, thus countering his "fear" by giving full vent to his "loathing." His characterizations of Hubert Humphrey earned him the indignant reproach of Stewart Alsop in *Newsweek*.[22] And, somewhat ruefully but with perceptible glee, he includes the tale of how he turned over his press credentials to a mysterious man he calls the Boohoo, who then used them to board the Muskie train in Florida and proceeded to terrorize the candidate and his retinue (pp. 103-15). These roguish tactics enable Dr. Thompson to survive in an environment which induces extreme psychic pressure. He is most playfully virulent when contemplating his worst fears. Realizing that the Democratic party might not offer a true alternative to Nixon, he entertains the possibility of "turning 50,000 bats loose in the Convention Center on the night of Hubert Humphrey's nomination" (p. 114). And when a callous young woman on a motor scooter forces her way through a march of maimed Vietnam Veterans against the War outside the Republican convention, he is "tempted to lean over and set her hair on fire with my Zippo" (p. 392). These fantasies, like the violent rhetoric, enable the persona mentally to confront events that he cannot actually alter.

But as it becomes clear that the American electorate will turn overwhelmingly toward an affirmation of the bestial side of its nature, Thompson increasingly portrays his persona as unable to write coherent reports and as prone to hallucinatory nightmare. When Dr. Thompson attempts to report on the last days of the doomed McGovern campaign, he feels compelled to confess that, on the day before, "suddenly my head rolled back and my eyes glazed over and I felt myself sucked into an irresistible time-warp." This time-warp does not allow him a Tralfamadorian escape, like those of Billy Pilgrim in *Slaughterhouse-Five*; rather, it brings about a surreal vision which combines his various journalistic experiences (he had previously written about the Kentucky Derby and motorcycle gangs):

I was standing at the bar in the clubhouse at Churchill Downs on Derby Day with Ralph Steadman, and we were drinking Mint Juleps at a pretty good pace, watching the cream of Bluegrass Society getting drunker and drunker out in front of us. . . . It was between races, and as I recall: Ralph was sketching and I was making notes ("3:45, Derby Day, standing at clubhouse bar now, just returned from Mens Room / terrible scene / whole place full of Kentucky Colonels vomiting into urinals & drooling bile down their seersucker pants-legs / Remind Ralph to watch for 'distinguished-looking' men in pari-mutuel lines wearing white-polished shoes with fresh vomit stains on the toes. . . .")

Right. We were standing there at the clubhouse bar, feeling very much on top of that boozy, back-slapping scene . . . when I suddenly glanced up from my notes & saw Frank Mankiewicz and Sonny Barger across the room, both of them wearing Hells Angels costumes and both holding heavy chrome chain whips . . . and yes, it was clear that they'd spotted us. Barger stared, not blinking, but Mankiewicz smiled his cold lizard's smile and they moved slowly through the drunken crowd to put themselves between us and the doorway. [pp. 420-21]

This vision brings together America's motorcycle outlaws, wealthy elite, and liberal politicians in a single parody of bestial behavior that proves too much for Dr. Thompson's consciousness. The November report must therefore be completed with the interview referred to earlier. The course of the campaign's actual events has fulfilled the paranoid fears of the persona, and the realization of these facts has temporarily disintegrated Dr. Thompson's personality. Having lost the ability to confer even a personal order upon the events, he must abandon his role as narrator, to become the subject of an editor's questions.

Dr. Thompson eventually recovers enough to write a subdued December chapter and an Epitaph. The first includes a postmortem interview with McGovern. (It should be noted here that, despite the emphasis on rhetoric and fantasy, *Campaign Trail* supplies considerable "news." [23]) The second ends with a Pynchonesque anti-detective parable of Dr. Thompson's activity after watching the Super Bowl in January:

Immediately after the game I received an urgent call from my attorney, who claimed to be having a terminal drug experience in his private bungalow at the Chateau Marmont . . . but by the time I got there he had finished the whole jar.

Later, when the big rain started, I got heavily into the gin and read the Sunday papers. On page 39 of *California Living* magazine I found a hand-lettered ad from the McDonald's Hamburger Corporation, one of Nixon's big contributors in the '72 presidential campaign:

PRESS ON, it said. NOTHING IN THE WORLD CAN TAKE THE PLACE OF PERSISTENCE. TALENT WILL NOT: NOTHING IS MORE COMMON THAN UNSUCCESSFUL MEN WITH TALENT. GENIUS WILL NOT: UNREWARDED GENIUS IS ALMOST A PROVERB. EDUCATION ALONE WILL NOT: THE WORLD IS FULL OF EDUCATED DERELICTS. PERSISTENCE AND DETERMINATION ALONE ARE OMNIPOTENT. [PP. 504–5]

In his disordered state, Dr. Thompson seems to feel that he has stumbled upon some important message in these clichés: "I read it several times before I grasped the full meaning. Then, when it came to me, I called Mankiewicz immediately. 'Keep your own counsel,' he said. 'Don't draw any conclusions from anything you see or hear' " (p. 505). This absurdist scene (one of a number that develop a recurring parody of the hardboiled detective form) presents the lesson Dr. Thompson has learned while on the campaign trail: the world is too permeated by false appearance, conspiracy, and delusion for one to trust the evidence of his senses. Since he can find no epistemological certainty in his contact with the macrocosm, Dr. Thompson retreats completely into the solipsistic solace of his own alienated consciousness: "I hung up and drank some more gin. Then I put a Dolly Parton album on the tape machine and watched the trees outside my balcony getting lashed around in the wind. Around midnight, when the rain stopped, I put on my special Miami Beach nightshirt and walked several blocks down La Cienega Boulevard to the Losers' Club" (p. 505). Combining elements of the Marx Brothers and Philip Marlowe to echo the ending of *A Farewell to Arms*, Thompson brings to an end the parodic allegory constructed by his persona's consciousness.

But the despair of the conclusion is not the conclusion itself, for the comic and inventive form counters the withdrawal, asserts the power of fable-making against the impotence of reporting. Dr. Thompson began the Epitaph parodying Grantland Rice's clichés before falling into a hallucination of mob violence at the Super Bowl, and then "waking" to compare the sportswriter's journalism to his own:

Gangs of Seconal-crazed teenagers prowled through the parking lot outside the stadium, beating the mortal shit out of luckless stragglers. . . .

What? No . . . . Grantland Rice would never have written weird stuff like that. . . . Like all great sportswriters, Rice understood that his world might go all to pieces if he ever dared to doubt that his eyes were wired straight to his lower brain—a sort of de facto lobotomy, which enables the grinning victim to operate entirely on the level of Sensory Perception. . . . [p. 500]

Dr. Thompson thus asserts that his fable-making is a necessary antidote to the prepackaged language, forms, and concepts with which the corporate media produce illusory images and abstractions. He has had to replace the detective role of the conventional reporter (based on the assumption of a rational, cause-and-effect world) with the artist role of the new journalist (based on a realization that the evidence of the macrocosm has already been artificially distorted and invented). Through his persona Thompson presents, however ironically, the need for private fable in the face of corporate fiction.

Following Mailer's example of creating literature dramatizing the attempt of an individual consciousness to comprehend a great event of contemporary American experience, Thompson has also drawn upon the techniques of the younger fabulist writers of the 1960's and 1970's to portray that struggle in the controlling mode of parody. Hyperbole, fantasy, and the tall tale all become literary embodiments of psychological defenses. His consciousness not merely reports, but also confronts great events. Thompson's writing is sometimes simply brutal or hip, but more often it offers a vision of the contemporary American landscape as serious and disturbed in its comedy as that of Vonnegut or Pynchon. And while it lacks the extraordinary inventiveness and complexity of the latter's fabulations, its power lies in its direct portrayals of actual events. Thompson has extended the possibilities of new journalism, and of contemporary literature in general.

5

Reporting the Fabulous:
Representation and Response
in the Work of Tom Wolfe

And it is an exceedingly strange feeling to be sitting here in the
Day-Glo, on poor abscessed Harriet Street, and realize suddenly that in this improbable ex-pie factory Warehouse garage I
am in the midst of Tsong-Ishapa and the sangha
communion . . .

—*The Electric Kool-Aid Acid Test*

Tom Wolfe has been the writer most completely identified with new journalism, both as practitioner and as spokes-
man. Originally he was attracted to the form by the journalistic
character studies that Gay Talese was writing for *Esquire* in the
early 1960's. At that time Wolfe, having completed a Ph.D. in
American Studies at Yale, was working as a reporter for the *New
York Herald Tribune*. He soon found himself going far beyond
the limits of conventional feature stories in attempts to deal with
the new phenomena to which his reporting brought him.[1] Since
publishing the first collection of his work, *The Kandy-Kolored
Tangerine-Flake Streamline Baby* (1965), he has continued to
produce articles and books at a rapid pace, perpetuating his
avowed aim of documenting the changing manners and morals
of contemporary American society. But while he has been the
writer who, among either journalists or novelists, has shown the
most willingness to deal with this topic, he has necessarily done
so less as a Balzac than as a Pynchon. For the consistent subject of
his reports on celebrities and subcultures has been the human
need to perceive and create patterns in a fragmenting society, and
his consistent theme has been the complex and often problematical relationship of those patterns to actuality.

With the exception of Mailer's journalistic contract in *The Executioner's Song*, Wolfe's version of that contract is in some ways stronger than those of the other new journalists considered here. Drawing both from the empirical methods on which Capote based his journalistic claims for *In Cold Blood* and from the metafictional assumptions on which Mailer and Thompson construct their autobiographical journalism, Wolfe is much more cautious in his application of these methods and assumptions. As a result, his works make far more modest claims for objective truth than *In Cold Blood*, but they avoid the solipsistic tendencies of *Of a Fire on the Moon* and *Fear and Loathing: On the Campaign Trail '72*. This caution increases the credibility of his journalistic contract and suggests his central thematic concern. Wolfe believes in both an objective actuality and subjective realities: "there is *not* just one reality, but there are certain things that are objectively known." [2] Thus he feels that the best art avoids an excessive emphasis on either external fact or internal fantasy:

The best thing is to have *both*—to have both someone who will bring you bigger and more exciting chunks of the outside world *plus* a unique sensibility, or rather a unique way of looking at the world, a unique fantasy life, even, to use the way Freud explains it, a unique emotional reality of his own that somehow echoes or vibrates with the emotional states of the reader. So that you get both the external reality and the subjective reality.

I'm not denying the existence of a subjective reality. Far from it. I'm just saying that there is also an objective reality that everyone in the world has to deal with. [3]

In order to make a contract with the reader which reflects this concept, Wolfe presents his works as carefully researched and factually verified reports shaped, interpreted, and dramatized through his personal vision. He seeks to avoid the solipsistic tendencies of Mailer's and Thompson's works by subduing his presence as a character and concentrating instead on the subject. But he also seeks to avoid the positivist tendencies of Capote's *In Cold Blood* by making his authorial presence a central reality of the work. His narrative stance is neither that of the fully dramatized first-person narrator and protagonist, nor that of the self-effacing omniscient author; rather, it is that of a human author with a unique sensibility, who has, through research and intellect, acquired extensive but nevertheless limited knowledge. He presents himself as neither a novelist nor an autobiographer, but as a working reporter and contemplative intellectual.

Wolfe's works are consistently composed of a combination of witnessed and reconstructed events. The journalistic contract he establishes reflects this by deriving its authority from his presence as either witnessing character or well-researched narrator. *The Electric Kool-Aid Acid Test*, typical of Wolfe's work in this respect, affords a good example for consideration. Just as Capote prefaces *In Cold Blood* with an acknowledgments page, so Wolfe frames his nonfiction novel with an "Author's Note," in an attempt to validate the factual nature of the work. Wolfe goes into much greater detail regarding his sources than did Capote, but he makes essentially the same claim: "All the events, details and dialogue I have recorded are either what I saw and heard myself or were told to me by people who were there themselves or were recorded on tapes or film or in writing." [4] But, unlike Capote, he has never proceeded in interviews to make claims of completely objective fact; rather, in the "Author's Note" he emphasizes that he has "tried not only to tell what the Pranksters did but to re-create the mental atmosphere or subjective reality of it" (p. 371). This suggests a different emphasis in his journalistic contract.

Even more important, in his technical approach to the narrative Wolfe applies this factual contract more cautiously than Capote did in *In Cold Blood*. The early and latter parts of *The Electric Kool-Aid Acid Test*, for instance, result from Wolfe's personal observations. Presenting these passages through his own eyes as a witness, he constructs them as fully dramatized scenes complete with extensive dialogue. But Wolfe constructs the bulk of the book's narrative, which is based on second-hand research, with far less dialogue and more thinly dramatized scenes. In these passages Wolfe relies far more on subjective description and feeling. This ontological shift, from dramatized scene complete with extensive dialogue to described scene dependent on impressionistic description, reflects the epistemological shift from first-hand observation to second-hand research. As a result, *The Electric Kool-Aid Acid Test* avoids one of the major weaknesses of *In Cold Blood*. Capote insisted on keeping himself completely out of a book which purported to represent an actual experience of which he came to be very much a part. This pretense had the strange effect of making those scenes which he had personally observed the least convincing in the book. And since both those events he constructed from first-hand observation and those he constructed from second-hand versions are dramatized through the same methods, the reader is left confused and doubtful regarding the book's credibility. Wolfe portrays himself as a witnessing character in those scenes representing events at which he was actually present, and he shifts his modes of narration to correspond to his modes of knowing. Thus he avoids these pitfalls and constructs a far more credible narrative.

Moreover, Wolfe presents his entire book through a narration which insists on its status as an individual creation and thus works from metafictional assumptions. Like Mailer and Thompson, he never lets the reader forget that his report of actual events is a construct of words composed by a human author, and that it is therefore as much an imaginative response to those events as it is a representation. Even when he is not presenting events through personal observations, he nevertheless continues to make his authorial presence felt. Intruding into the narrative at various points through a device he calls the Hectoring Narrator, Wolfe speaks conversationally to the reader ("I couldn't tell you what bright fellow thought of that, inviting Kesey"), and to his characters ("That's good thinking there, Cool Breeze") as a casual means of supplying his authorial reactions to the events he is describing. Such seemingly spontaneous interruptions of the narrative draw attention to Wolfe's mediating presence between the events and the reader. He also goes so far as to intrude at times in order to acknowledge the limits of his knowledge, with such disarmingly frank admissions as "I couldn't tell you for sure which of the Merry Pranksters got the idea for the bus, but . . ." and even simply, "I don't know." As Mas'ud Zavarzadeh has pointed out, "The epistemological effect of the typographical presence of the 'I' is the owning of a 'self,' and thus a warning to the reader that everything is told by a single man with his unique, acknowledged limitations." [5]

Even when he is not functioning as a first-person witness or intrusive narrator, Wolfe is highly present in a style so mannered and distinctive, even eccentric, that it has become a favorite object of reviewers' parodies. It is an insistently verbal and even iconic style which draws on the full rhythmic, onomatopoeic, and even visual potential of written language. Wolfe uses unusual punctuation, unconventional capitalization, esoteric words, and even narrative poetry. While they ostensibly aim to duplicate the experience of the events they refer to, they also remind the reader that he is in fact experiencing Wolfe's verbal construct of the experience, not the experience itself.

Committed by his complex journalistic contract to deal only in fact, Wolfe has been freed by this commitment to vent the full power of his imagination in his formal and stylistic presentation. Though he considers himself a practitioner of realism (confusing that mode with the goal of verisimilitude), he has in fact used his journalistic contract to escape the formal and stylistic restrictions under which the realist labors. That contract enables him to ignore the latter's concern with plausibility and objectivity. With his strong journalistic contract, Wolfe has no need to restrict himself to the relatively "styleless" conventions and middle-range subjects by which the realist attempts to gain an illusion of reality. He is instead free to narrate in a style which attempts far more than neutral representation. In his desire to report his actual subjects in terms of their subjective realities and underlying patterns, Wolfe has developed a wide range of innovative formal and stylistic devices. The result, while often excessively mannered and "glittering," at its best embodies a uniquely effective application of the kind of experimental literary technique associated with the avant-garde to the reportorial content claimed by conventional journalists and realists.

The most pervasive and striking aspect of Wolfe's approach is its assertive character. From his use of point of view to his choice of descriptive words, Wolfe is continually seeking to *respond* to the actuality, not just to represent it. We have already noted his use of the Hectoring Narrator, which he says he devised because "I liked the idea of starting off a story by letting the reader, via the narrator, talk to the characters, hector them, insult them, prod them with irony or condescension, or whatever. Why should the reader be expected to just lie flat and let these people come tromping through as if his mind were a subway turnstile? " [6] Even when Wolfe does not use such directly intrusive devices, his insistent choices of hyperbolic, kinetic, or baroque words and phrases make his descriptions as much an assault as a representation.

His style is characterized by consistently violent description (sunlight on glasses or windshields always "explodes"), an almost fetishistic use of certain esoteric words ("sclerotic" and "infarcted" are favorites), a love of terms which are either jarringly clinical or unusually figurative ("gluteus maximi" and "mary poppins"), and a frequent catalogue of brand names and descriptions of synthetic fabrics by specific names (girls wear "Tiger Tongue Lick Me brush-on eyelashes," and a woman dresses in "diaphanous polyethylene"). He also likes to fragment his panoramic descriptions by impressionistic use of synecdoche, suggesting sensory overload, as in this view of an audience of girls at a 1964 Rolling Stones concert:

Bangs manes bouffants beehives Beatle caps butter faces brush-on lashes decal eyes puffy sweaters French thrust bras flailing leather blue jeans stretch pants stretch jeans honeydew bottoms eclair shanks elf boots ballerinas Knight slippers, hundreds of them, these flaming little buds, bobbing and screaming, rocketing around inside the Academy of Music Theater underneath that vast old mouldering cherub dome up there—aren't they super-marvelous! [7]

These stylistic traits work like those of the cubists to break up the reader's usual modes of perception. One of his style's major strengths is that it not only represents the appearance but also conveys the fabulous character of the subject. While contemporary writers of realistic fiction have labored with mixed success to solve the dilemma of how to make a fabulous reality seem real, Wolfe, working from the relatively assured credibility of his factual contract, has been able to represent contemporary phenomena in full detail while emphasizing the effect of strangeness. By portraying strange phenomena through strange prose, he retains and even heightens the fabulous quality of the actuality he is reporting. As a result, his chronicles seem, even in substance, to be fables.

Wolfe's formal techniques also result from the freedom of his journalistic contract and are prompted by the need to respond to actuality. This is most apparent in the overall make-up of his works. Despite the excessive theoretical significance he has placed on his use of scenic construction in new journalism, his more revealing comments have emphasized the value of the new journalists' willingness to experiment, claiming that "their innocence has kept them free." [8] Indeed, his story about writing his first new journalistic article emphasized its informal, letter-like composition (see Chapter I). And in his account of the writing of his nonfiction novel, *The Electric Kool-Aid Acid Test*, he tells how he finally abandoned strict reliance on scenes:

Up until that point I had also been held back by the question of technique. Now I just started writing flat out, doing 10 to 20 pages a day at some stretches, writing scene by scene where I had material, but going into straight exposition where that came more naturally. The main thing was just to get it all down. Yet suddenly I found myself using techniques I had never even thought about before, including narrative poems.[9]

The works themselves—with their lengthy passages of authorial analysis and meditation, often dramatized as an unfolding intuitive process—show that Wolfe, although he certainly does use the whole range of fictional devices, is finally not relying mainly on the techniques of realistic fiction. Rather, he is experimenting with a new form in which, as he has said, "there are really no traditions . . . worth observing." [10]

But if new journalism, and most particularly that written by Tom Wolfe, is as much a break from realistic fiction as it is from conventional journalism, one must ask why Wolfe insists that it is the *ultimate* realism, and the vital alternative to an effetely irrelevant contemporary fiction. Wolfe's assertions in interviews and in the notorious introduction to *The New Journalism* can be better understood, I think, if they are viewed in relation to Poe's "Philosophy of Composition" and Zola's "Experimental Novel." Both of these aesthetic self-justifications were prompted by the authors' desires to gain more serious readings for their works and are notorious misrepresentations of the artists' true methods and achievements. Poe's incredible tale of his methodical composition of "The Raven" was probably a hyperbolic effort, as Robert Jacobs has put it, at "attempting to refute the idea that artistic genius and skill were incompatible [and] if Poe overstated the case for deliberate procedure, it was because he had to use everything he could to combat the transcendentalists, who made the artist the passive vehicle of Divine Truth." [11] Likewise, Zola's "Experimental Novel" made impossible claims for his fiction-writing. Assertions that it is the literary counterpart of laboratory experiments are, fortunately, belied by the magnificently surreal and mythic novels themselves. Nevertheless, Zola clearly felt the need to gain the sanction and power of objective science for his work. Thus both of these aesthetic essays can best be understood only if we take them, not at face value, but as positionings for strategic advantage.

Wolfe's "New Journalism" manifesto should be read with similar skepticism. On the one hand, Wolfe had been severely attacked by Dwight Macdonald in *The New York Review of Books* for being a "parodist" who allegedly has "fewer inhibitions about accuracy than obtains in the more reputable public relations firms." The factual claims of his *New Yorker* pieces had been subjected by both Macdonald and the *Columbia Journalism Review* to excruciatingly detailed autopsies. [12] Wolfe must have felt that his all-important contract as a reporter was in severe danger. (Some of his comments in the essay indicate that these attacks were indeed on his mind, and that he perceived them as aimed at new journalism in general. [13]) On the other hand, he apparently felt threatened by the fabulators' exaltation of pure invention and form. Responding with an aesthetic manifesto which stressed his function as a meticulous reporter using traditional fictional techniques, he asserted the superiority of his supposed "realism" to both the rigid formulas of conventional journalists and the private fantasies of fabulators. [14] The result is a theoretical travesty which should be read not for its claims, but for its underlying motivations: the need to protect the all-important author-reader contract of dealing in actual fact, and the desire to acquire literary status for an imaginative form too easily dismissed as mere reportage.

Wolfe's most important works have been his two novel-length studies of hero figures and their relations to distinct periods of change in the American culture of the 1960's. *The Right Stuff* (1979) is a finely wrought and extensively researched, if relatively subdued, account of the transformation of test pilots into the astronaut-heroes of a media-dominated age of symbolic warfare with the Soviet Union. His most complexly experimental (if less successfully controlled) work, *The Electric Kool-Aid Acid Test* (1968), is an account of Ken Kesey's role in the origins and early history of the psychedelic movement.[15] Because *The Right Stuff* is, in stylistic and formal terms, a more conservative and cautious practice of the devices and structures developed most strikingly and innovatively in *The Electric Kool-Aid Acid Test*, I have selected the latter for close analysis. Wolfe originally came upon the material when he went to San Francisco in order to research a *Herald Tribune* story on the arrest, flight, and then sudden recapture of Ken Kesey, the author of *One Flew Over the Cuckoo's Nest* (1962) and *Sometimes a Great Notion* (1964). Soon, however, he found that he had a much larger story on his hands. After publishing two articles, which Wolfe considers "thin stuff" and which caused him the embarrassment of Kesey's faint praise, he continued his research. According to his own account, he then returned to Virginia and wrote the book in a four-month marathon.[16]

The action of *The Electric Kool-Aid Acid Test* follows the rise of the hallucinogenic drug culture in California during the 1960's and the corresponding rise and fall of Kesey as its chief leader and theorist. It begins and ends with the activities of Kesey and his followers, the Merry Pranksters, in San Francisco while he was free on bail after his apprehension as a fugitive. Wolfe personally witnessed these scenes, but the preponderance of the narrative is told in one long flashback. Wolfe traces Kesey's life from his first experiences with LSD as a volunteer subject in the early 1960's to his recapture in late 1966. Despite its detail, Wolfe creates far more than a document in this book. While *The Electric Kool-Aid Acid Test* is the most thorough and insightful report on the rise of the counterculture in California in the 1960's, it is also a powerful portrayal of a quintessentially American quest. Ultimately, it is Wolfe's exploration of the relationship of that quest to actuality, and of both to the book itself.

Previous discussion of *The Electric Kool-Aid Acid Test* has nearly always focused upon Wolfe's unique style, or else has treated the book as a mere documentary account of Ken Kesey's artistic experiment with life. In the following pages I intend to study one particular aspect of Wolfe's artistic handling of his factual material in order to show how he creates a documentary that possesses the larger significance of a fable. While using material drawn only from interviews, tapes, letters, and personal observation, Wolfe consciously uses language to transform his facts into shapes with a fabulist resonance. More particularly, he uses allusions to classic American literature to suggest the larger patterns within which he perceives the factual narrative to be unfolding. Wolfe draws upon a number of classic American literary works in *The Electric Kool-Aid Acid Test*, but he causes the reader to view its climactic events through the lenses of Poe's short story "A Descent into the Maelstrom." The highly stylized and allusive structure of his narrative draws attention to itself as a pattern; it functions clearly as a thematic overlay, the product of Wolfe's interpretive consciousness standing outside of the factual events. The power of *The Electric Kool-Aid Acid Test* lies in this dynamic balance between the fictive nature of its created form and the factual nature of its content.

After chronicling his own initiation into the Haight-Ashbury culture that Ken Kesey had helped to create, Tom Wolfe begins the main narrative of *The Electric Kool-Aid Acid Test* by presenting Kesey's memories of his youth in post–World War II American suburbia. Wolfe shows that Kesey is a product of the postwar culture which believed it had at last discovered how to realize the American Dream. Through abundant money and technology, Americans were able to revel in the freedom and adventure they had always craved. Wolfe finds a perfect symbol for this new vision of the classic Dream in Kesey's childhood memory of "the radio tower of station KORE with a red light blinking on top." He could see it far behind his house when he knelt and said his prayers, so that "there would be the sky and the light blinking—and he always kind of thought he was praying to that red light" (pp. 33–34). Wolfe's presentation of Kesey's prayerful relationship to the blinking red light atop the radio station inevitably recalls that of Gatsby outstretching his arms to the green light on Daisy's dock. For Kesey and the postwar generation, the Dream seems at last attainable—no longer through nature, but through its technological alteration. This is the first of a number of allusions by which Wolfe places his account of Kesey's actual journey in the tradition of American literary quests. His subsequent description of Kesey's memory of automobiles crashing into a ditch night after night, as their drivers confusedly pursued the red light ("praying to the red beacon light of KORE!"), is his first suggestion of its ultimate folly. (The switch from a green to a red light suggests, of course, a warning—not perceived by Kesey—that it is really time to move from "go" to "stop" in pursuit of the Dream.)

Kesey's belief that actuality is a malleable fantasy (p. 29) was already embedded in his mind when, as an aspiring young writer living in an artists' colony called Perry Lane, he met a young Viennese analyst who introduced him to Freudian psychology and hallucinogenic drug experiments at a nearby Veterans Hospital. These latter two influences suggested to Kesey that life is a complex metaphor changing with modes of perception. As Wolfe portrays Kesey's developing philosophy, Kesey becomes convinced that the barrier between the subjective and objective is illusory and can be bridged in "a life in which the subject is not scholastic or bureaucratic but . . . *Me* and *Us,* the *attuned* ones amid the non-musical shiny-black-shoe multitudes, *I*-with my eyes on that almost invisible *hole* up there in the r-r-r-redwood sky. . ." (p. 58). With this goal he uses his considerable personal charisma and literary earnings to set up a loose community, later to be known as the Merry Pranksters, in a redwood forest near La Honda in 1964.

Wolfe views Kesey as an embodiment of the American drive to attain perfect freedom and oneness with experience, as well as a religious figure seeking to attain the oriental idea of breaking through the illusory barrier between the subjective and objective. The combination of these two drives, of course, is not new. Through allusion Wolfe tells us that Kesey's transformation of Perry Lane is viewed by visitors as "Walden Pond, only without any Thoreau misanthropes around" (p. 47). Wolfe thus suggests that Kesey's quest has direct precedent in that of the American transcendentalists. His desire to eliminate all "lags" between experience and sensory perception, so as to embrace all experience in an eternal Now in which the objective and subjective are dissolved into one transcendent experience, as well as his impatience with craft in art in favor of a principle of organic form (Kesey stopped writing in favor of more fluid and less artificial forms), echoes Emerson's desire to become a "transparent eyeball." The crucial distinction is that Kesey seeks this state not through nature but through technology. That distinction is obvious in his later version of Walden at La Honda, where he has redwood trees outfitted with music speakers and spiderwebs sprayed with Day-Glo paint.

The drug-induced concept of the sky as a hole reaching into an infinity of possible experience, combined with the postwar American belief that technology can make any fantasy possible, leads Kesey to organize the Pranksters into painting a bus in a lurid mess of primary colors, flying American flags from the top, equipping it with an audio-visual technology, and then taking it on a cross-country adventure. They transform the bus into an embodiment of Kesey's desire to pursue the American Dream to its furthest limits through the unashamed alteration of nature (over the windshield he places the name of their destination as "Furthur"). After a brief trial run, the Pranksters set out east, reversing the traditional western trek. Their journey signals the end of one frontier, but not the end of the search itself. Most of the first half of *Test* follows Kesey's attainment of a messiah-like status among the Pranksters as he teaches them to assert their private "fantasies" against the rigid "reality" of the dominant culture. Eventually he conceives of the Acid Tests—dances to be held in San Francisco and, later, Los Angeles—in order to bring the larger society into his vision of a transcendent life attained through LSD and technology.

Immediately before his narration of the first Acid Test midway through the narrative, Wolfe refers to one of the books the Pranksters revered, saying that "The Acid Tests turned out, in fact, to be an art form foreseen in that strange book, *Childhood's End*, a form called 'total identification' " (p. 208). This reference is to Arthur C. Clarke's science-fiction vision of an art form in which all senses would be stimulated to the point that a person could mentally participate in any experience. Wolfe quotes from Clarke's description: "And when the 'program' was over, he would have acquired a memory as vivid as any experience in his actual life—indeed, indistinguishable from reality itself" (p. 208). Wolfe follows this quotation with an ominously intrusive comment, "Too freaking true!" (p. 208). Sarcastic use of the Pranksters' hip phrasing indicates the fatal error that he believes is behind the doom toward which Kesey's quest is moving. For Wolfe, as for the dark romantic authors of classic American literature, the inability to distinguish fact from fantasy in a reverie of transcendent experience is a profound error leading to dissolution of the self.

At this point in the narrative, as he is about to begin the story of the Acid Tests, Wolfe makes clear allusions which suggest that the reader should view these events in the framework of a classic work of American literature, one dealing with a true plunge into a vortex, Poe's " Descent into the Maelstrom." It is not surprising that Wolfe, with his sociologist's belief in facts and analysis as well as his skepticism toward the viability of a purely subjective reality, should use a story by one of the great dark romantics as the metaphorical framework for the climactic chapters of his Kesey narrative. Poe presents "A Descent into the Maelstrom" as an oral tale once told by a fisherman to the narrator, who now presents it to us in the fisherman's own words. As they stand at the edge of a cliff above a horrifying oceanic whirlpool, the "maelstrom," the fisherman tells his tale of having been accidentally swept into the swirling vortex. Eric W. Carlson has provided a succinct interpretation of the story's significance:

The whirlpool is Poe's most obsessive image of the human condition: in a heedless universe man is swept down in fear and dread to almost certain death. In "A Descent into the Maelstrom," wishing to see a great manifestation of God's power, the protagonist passes, from his resignation to imminent death, to a curiosity to explore the depths of the maelstrom; but when, his wish granted, the moonlight penetrates deep down into the Abyss, out of the mist and the rainbow there rises a terrifying, an indescribable shriek. If he lives to tell the tale, he does so as another ancient mariner, unnerved and greatly aged by his experience.[17]

Wolfe introduces this motif in his description of the third Acid Test. As he describes approximately 300 "heads" gathered on the floor, well into LSD trips and about to experience the Pranksters' projection of "The Movie" and a psychedelic light show upon the walls, Wolfe sums up the moment with the allusive exclamation, "Into the maelstrom!" (p. 215). His subsequent narration of the night's events develops this motif through the central imagery of Poe's story. He describes the setting as a chaotic ocean of experience which the Pranksters have contrived through audio-visual technology:

The Movie and Roy Seburn's light machine pitching the intergalactic red science-fiction seas to all corners of the lodge, oil and water and food coloring pressed between plates of glass and projected in vast size so that the very ooze of cellular Creation seems to ectoplast into the ethers and then the Dead coming in with their immense submarine vibrato vibrating, *garanging*, from the Aleutian rocks to the baja griffin cliffs of the Gulf of California. [p. 216]

Wolfe describes the experience of a man sucked into the developing maelstrom of the Acid Test:

into *the whirlpool* who should appear but Owsley. Owsley, done up in his $600 head costume, has emerged from his subterrain of espionage and paranoia to come to see the Prankster experiment for himself, and in the middle of the giddy contagion he takes LSD. They never saw him take it before. He takes the LSD and
RRRRRRRRRRRRRRRRRRRRRRRROIL
the whirlpool picks him up and spins him down into the stroboscopic stereoptic prankster panopticon in full variable lag [p. 216; italics mine]

As Owsley is swept into the whirling abyss of the LSD experience, Wolfe switches to Kesey, who

Looks out upon the stroboscopic whirlpool—the dancers! flung and flinging! *in ecstasis*! gyrating! levitating! men in slices! in pingpong balls! in the creamy bare essence and it reaches a
SYNCH
he never saw before. Heads from all over the acid world out here and *all whirling into the pudding* [italics mine]. Now let a man see what

CONTROL

is. Kesey mans the strobe and a twist of the mercury lever

UP

and they all speed up

NOW

the whole whirlpool, so far into it, they are. Faster they dance, hands thrown up off their arms like confetti in the strobe flashing, blissful faces falling apart and being exchanged, for I am you and you are me in Cosmo's Tasmanian deviltry. Turn it

DOWN

and they slow down—or We turn down—It—Cosmo—turns down, still in perfect synch, one brain, one energy, a single flow of intersubjectivity. It is *possible*, this alchemy so dreamed of by all the heads. It is happening before them

CONTROL [pp. 217-18]

As Wolfe describes this scene, it is clear that Kesey has taken on the role of God, created a reality from his private fantasy in which he views others as trapped. Wolfe next describes the feeling of being "into the still of the hurricane, the pudding" (p. 218), which follows the night's frenzy. This passage represents the temporary attainment of Kesey's transcendent goal; it also parallels the passage in the Poe story where the fisherman temporarily feels blissful indifference to his imminent destruction as he watches this "manifestation of God's power."

But he then switches back to Owsley at dawn. He has returned from the LSD trip—just as the fisherman returned from the whirlpool—"lurching and groping and screaming 'Survival!'" (p. 219). Wolfe recounts that, after Owsley "got caught in the whirlpool" (p. 219) of the LSD and the Pranksters' special effects, he had the terrifying experience of dissolving:

The whole world was coming to pieces molecule by molecule now and swimming like grease bubbles in a cup of coffee, disappearing into the intergalactic ooze and gasses all around—including his own body. He lost his skin, his skeleton, his pulmonary veins—sneaking out into the ooze like eels, they are, reeking phosphorus, his neural ganglia—unraveling like hot worms and wiggling down the galactic drain, his whole substance dissolving into gaseous nothingness until finally he was down to one cell. *One human cell*: his; that was all that was left of the entire known world, and if he lost control of that one cell, there would be nothing left. [p. 220]

He "survives" this experience, a negative version of the blissful "intersubjectivity" that Kesey seeks, only after jumping into a car and smashing it into a tree that he thought no longer existed: "But the crash somehow pops the whole world back. There it is; back from the fat-bubbling ooze. The car is smashed, but he has survived" (p. 221). After surviving, however, Owsley becomes "obsessed" with the experience of his descent into the whirlpool of the Acid Test; like the fisherman, he endlessly recounts the story, for "it seemed to horrify and intrigue him at the same time—such morbid but wonderful details" (p. 222).

The Acid Tests are the culmination of Kesey's attempt to break through to a total embrace of experience through technology (both the chemical LSD and the projected light show and electronic music). But as he sees himself successfully projecting his fantasy experience to others, he is assuming the dangerous role of seeing his will as more powerful than actuality. Wolfe's perception of the satanic element of this role is apparent in the chapter title, "Cosmo's Tasmanian Deviltry" (a phrase he shows moving through Kesey's thoughts as he controls the flashing strobe-light at the Acid Test), and in his emphasis upon Owsley's new view of Kesey as a "demon" (p. 222). When Wolfe later recounts the "Trips Festival," which Kesey attends just before his flight to Mexico, he returns to the Poe allusion, describing Kesey with a projection machine on a balcony above the hall as "up above the maelstrom" (p. 232). At one point Kesey uses the projector to flash a message in red on the wall: "ANYBODY WHO KNOWS HE IS GOD GO UP ON STAGE" (p. 234). Kesey believes that he stands safely above the maelstrom, on an edge of perfect control. This "edge," which is a metaphor Kesey often uses to describe the goal of the Pranksters' quest to transcend the distinction between subjective and objective reality, is portrayed by Wolfe, as by Poe and Melville, as a dangerous position inducing a cosmic vertigo. He repeatedly emphasizes Kesey's position as one high above the affairs of the world. This position provides him with the vantage point, "the conning tower" (p. 290), of an overview of experience—as well as with the illusion of being safely distant from its dangers. But that illusion inevitably leads to his succumbing to the danger of such a position—a fall into the whirlpool of actual experience below. While Kesey believes he is in control and standing above the maelstrom, Wolfe shows that he is in fact already caught in the whirlpool and is descending, like Owsley, into the dissolving "ooze" in the vortex of experience.

Wolfe develops this pattern in a number of scenes in the second half of *The Electric Kool-Aid Acid Test*. The first portrays Kesey's second arrest for possession of marijuana two nights before the Trips Festival. This arrest occurs while Kesey and Mountain Girl are perched high above San Francisco on the roof of an apartment building. High both physically and mentally, they watch with blissful indifference as a police car pulls up far below:

The cops are coming in this building. Wonder on earth what for. *Do I learn anything? Or once again lie loaded and disbelieving as two cops climb five stories to drag me to the cooler* . . . Oh, the logic of the groove and the synch. Kesey and Mountain Girl see it all at once, now, so clearly. It is so very obvious that it fascinates. They see it all, grok it all—*Scram, split, run, flee, hide, vanish, disintegrate*—the red alert is so very clear, it blinks and blinks, red, nothing, red, nothing, red, nothing, red, nothing, and yet *move?* and *miss it all?* turning so slow in the interferrometric synch? [pp. 228-29]

For the reader who recalls the blinking red light that Kesey had felt he was praying to in his youth, the red light which symbolized Kesey's pursuit of technological fulfillment of the American Dream, Wolfe's description of Kesey watching the police car's light repeatedly blinking "red, nothing" has ominous significance. And Wolfe's previous use of the whirlpool image lends an equally ominous significance to the feeling of "turning so slow in the interferrometric synch." Indeed, Wolfe proceeds to show that the resulting arrest, which increases the likelihood of a lengthy prison sentence for Kesey, leads him after the Trips Festival to descend geographically to the southwestern tip of Mexico, in a journey that is paralleled by a psychological descent into deeper fantasy.

Wolfe uses this dual descent as the structural and thematic principle of "The Fugitive" chapter. Drawing on interviews with Kesey as well as on the extensive letters, notes, and tapes Kesey made at the time, Wolfe portrays Kesey's growing paranoia through a stream-of-consciousness interior monologue as he sits in a rented room on the west coast of Mexico, convinced that FBI agents are about to enter. Wolfe alternates this descent into unreality with an account of Kesey's journey through the Mexican desert into this spot in the jungle, describing it as a movement "into total nothing, like the lines of perspective in a surrealist painting" (p. 260).

The effect of Wolfe's alternating narrative is to unite the physical and fantasy flights in a single escape from actuality, culminating in Kesey's paranoid leap over the back wall into the unreal "picturebook jungles of Mexico" (p. 267) as he imagines that the FBI agents are coming up the stairs. The person who actually enters is only a Prankster, but Kesey spends hours hiding in the jungle, alternately consumed by paranoia and by megalomania, first surrounding himself with DDT to ward off the jungle insects and then exerting his will to draw them into his power. In either case, he has descended into a world of fantasy that seems increasingly unrelated to the facts of his situation.

In the next chapter Wolfe makes extensive use of an invented voice as a narrative device which personifies the reaction of the local Mexicans to Kesey and the Pranksters. With the arrival of the Pranksters, a "red tide" of multiplying plankton has turned the sea crimson and killed the fish. The voice identifies the gaudy colors of the "devilish bus" with the red tide and believes that the Pranksters come from it:

—one vast immortal Group Animicula, fifteen miles long and three miles wide, immortal, in truth. The first little *Gymnodinium brevis* still lives just as surely as the 128-billionth as the red tide spreads. For they increase simply by cell division. The great marlins die, the porpoises, all the creatures of the sea die, and the fishermen die, but the *Gymnodinium* is immortal, the instant brother of every *Gymnodinium brevis* who ever lived, no past, no future, only Now and immortal, the little fockers. No *cause*, senor, no *starting point* in time, just the point at which your game intersected the 256-octillionth *Gymnodinium* and all his ancestors and successors in old Manzanillo and brought you up tight. We know only that yesterday there were fish, and today the fish are dead and the poison plankton and the American crazies are alive, and tomorrow we must find out the cause and the cure—or could it *possibly* be that yesterday and tomorrow are merely more of Now stretching fifteen miles and three miles wide immortal— [p. 280]

This description is a malignant version of Kesey's quest to obtain a perfect oneness with the world and with others. In addition, Wolfe has foreshadowed the red color earlier by his portrayal of the "red light" on top of the radio station, as well as by his emphatic description of the light on top of the police car. Even more suggestively, Kesey and the Pranksters projected "red seas" on the walls at the Acid Tests. The perception of the red tide as "one vast immortal Group Animicule" has likewise been foreshadowed by Owsley's LSD-induced nightmare of the world dissolving into a single entropic "ooze" ending in only "one cell." Wolfe's presentation of the Mexican voice's reaction to the red tide suggests that the transcendent unity of experience which Kesey seeks is a nothingness.

Wolfe shows Kesey in Mexico continuing to alternate between paranoia and megalomania, with the latter gradually coming to dominate his fantasies as he begins to conceive of himself as a secret agent who will defiantly reenter America: "The current fantasy was to take the Outlaw prank to its ultimate, be a Prankster Fugitive Extraordinaire in the Baskin-Robbins bosom of the U.S.A." (p. 307). As Wolfe narrates it, Kesey succeeds in a Hollywood-movie escape from the Mexican police, again crossing the border in outlandish disguise. But these fabulous adventures only increase his fantasy life; he comes to think of his relationship with the FBI in California as a "Cops and Robbers Game" (p. 311) in which he becomes "a kind of Day-Glo Pimpernel" (p. 312).

Wolfe eventually brings this game into proper perspective by juxtaposing Kesey's fantasy version of "the grand finale" with the actual arrest. Kesey envisions a masked Test in which he will appear in a Super-Hero costume and deliver his "vision of the future":

Then he will rip off his mask—*Why—it's Ken Kee-zee!*—and as the law rushes for him, he will leap up on a rope hanging down from the roof at center stage and climb, hand over hand, without even using his legs, with his cape flying, straight up, up, up through a trap door in the roof, to where Babbs will be waiting with a helicopter, Captain Midnight of the U.S. Marines, and they will ascend into the California ozone looking down one last time into the upturned moon faces of all the put-on, nonplused, outwitted, befuddled befreaked *shucked*! constables and sleuths Yeah! Yeah! Right! Right! Right! (p. 328)

Wolfe immediately follows Kesey's fantasy of ascension (which recalls his desire to go through the hole of infinite experience he saw in the sky) with the factual arrest, an actual fulfillment—as Wolfe selects the details and language—of Owsley's account of his mental "descent into the maelstrom." Trapped on the highway by the FBI as he rides with a fellow Prankster, Kesey runs down an embankment which leads to a drain. Viewing the scene through the witnessing Prankster's eyes, Wolfe emphasizes a detail of the setting which is resonant with irony:

On the other side of the expressway, on the edge of the bay, great fat seagulls *are wheeling in the air in a great weird O pattern*, coasting down below the level of the highway, then struggling up, dripping garbage out of their gullets, but a nice pattern, all in all—
    THE VISITACION DRAIN
It's the Visitacion Drain they've picked to work out their karma in . . . ah, we're synched up this afternoon . . . and the gulls wax fat gulping garbage at the drain and grease a slippery fat O in the sky and it occurs to Hassler that today is his twenty-seventh birthday [p. 330; italics mine]

The O pattern formed by the circling birds suggests the whirlpool motif, an ironic image of the "big hole" in the sky that Kesey had initially perceived as a route to infinite experience and through which he has just fantasized his ascension. It seems now to represent the nothingness to which his quest has led him as he descends into the drain, a "vortex" of modern America's waste.

    Wolfe's description of this descent effectively combines both the fantasy and actuality of the experience, while also investing it with the symbolic impact of the maelstrom motif:

    Skidding down the embankment chocking up dust like in a Western the blur of the Drain flats out beyond Kesey vaults over an erosion fence at the bottom of the embankment
    Ri-i-i-i-i-ip
a picket catches his pants in the crotch rips out the in-seams of both pants legs most neatly flapping on his legs like Low Rent cowboy chaps running and flapping through the Visitacion flats poor petered-out suckmuck marginal housing development last blasted edge of land you

can build houses on before they just sink into the ooze and the compost
poor Visitacion Drain kids playing ball in the last street before the ooze
runs flapping through their ballgame stare at him
    AND AT THE GHOST ON MY HEELS?
like the whole world turns into an endless kids' ballgame on the edge of
the ooze thousands of Drain kids furling toward the horizon like an
urchin funnel
    AND THAT ALUMICRON BLUR BEHIND ME?
shiny black shoes tusking up behind him stops stock still in the Visitacion Drain and
    GOTCHA!
in the cops and robbers game. [p. 331]

The "ooze" of the garbage that Wolfe so repetitively emphasizes
as the bottom of this symbolic vortex recalls Owsley's LSD vision
of the world as dissolving into "pieces molecule by molecule now
and swimming like grease bubbles . . . into the intergalactic
ooze . . . wiggling down the galactic drain, his whole substance
dissolving into gaseous nothingness" (p. 220). In this drain Kesey
finds the end of his quest to go ever "Furthur," finds the "last
blasted edge." With the confusing merger of words in the stream-
of-consciousness description, Wolfe suggests that Kesey himself
has become nothing, the "ooze" that Owsley experienced: "in
the last street before the ooze runs flapping through their ballgame stare at him." Owsley's "bad trip" on LSD has become the
actuality of the end of Kesey's quest. Kesey has symbolically met
the annihilation that Poe's fisherman glimpsed but pulled back
from in horror. In the ensuing chapters Wolfe shows that Kesey is
unable to control or even direct the fantasy he started, the new
Haight-Ashbury drug culture.

The main theme of Wolfe's book is the inevitable doom of
Kesey's attempt to embrace all experience by going completely
beyond confining patterns. An important subtheme, however,
deals with this folly in art and communication. Since Wolfe's
book obviously attempts to deal meaningfully with experience
through a highly patterned and unashamedly verbal construct, it
should not be surprising that Wolfe demonstrates some concern
for Kesey's attitudes toward artistic representation of experience. He reminds the reader that Kesey has stopped writing in

favor of making his life a work of art, and of capturing more experience in the experimental movie the Pranksters are making of their adventures. Kesey objects to literature because writers "are trapped by artificial rules" (p. 136). In his desire to embrace all experience and then to communicate pure expression to others, he has become disillusioned with the artifice involved in adherence to any conventions. The problem with this approach, Wolfe suggests in his description of the Pranksters' work on their movie, is that, without the artifice of conventions, communication becomes problematical:

There were very few establishing shots, shots showing where the bus was when this or that took place. But who needs that old Hollywood thing of long shot, medium shot, closeup, and the careful cuts and wipes and pans and dolly in and dolly out, the old bullshit. Still . . . plunging in on those miles of bouncing, ricocheting, blazing film with a splicer was like entering a jungle where the greeny vines grew faster than you could chop them down in front of you. [p. 122]

The jungle image recurs later in Wolfe's narrative as symbolic of Kesey's state of chaotic fantasy, and Wolfe's use of it here suggests a connection between the problems of fantasy as an approach to life and the problems of pure expression as an approach to art. By implication, Wolfe is suggesting the need for artifice in any viable communication.

Wolfe's artistic disagreements in *The Electric Kool-Aid Acid Test* are not only with Kesey, any more than in his theoretical statements they are only with the fabulators. Wolfe has been equally adamant in his attacks on conventional journalism. A minor theme running throughout this work is the comic inability of the media to capture even part of the truth of the subject on which it reports. In fact, he portrays their error as worse than Kesey's, for whereas Kesey conveys too much of the experience to provide any meaningful pattern, the conventional media convey a complete misrepresentation of the experience through the rigid imposition of irrelevant pattern. If Kesey's error is an excess of formlessness, the media's is an excess of form. Both fail to find a proper combination between objective actuality and subjective pattern.

As Wolfe portrays the media, their representatives always

come to an event with a predetermined concept of its reality and rigidly force the experience to fit that concept. Wolfe's portrayal of the press's description of the destruction of Perry Lane, which he presents in a parody of the brief news column, comically reveals the inadequacy of conventional journalism's preestablished forms and ideas:

PALO ALTO, CALIF., July 21, 1963—and then one day the end of an era, as the papers like to put it. A developer bought most of Perry Lane and was going to tear down the cottages and put up modern houses and the bulldozers were coming.

The papers turned up to write about the last night on Perry Lane, noble old Perry Lane, and had the old cliché at the ready, End of an Era, expecting to find some deep-thinking latter-day Thorstein Veblen intellectuals on hand with sonorous bitter statements about this machine civilization devouring its own past.

Instead, there were some kind of *nuts* out here. They were up in a tree lying on a mattress, all high as coons, and they kept offering everybody, all the reporters and photographers, some kind of venison chili, but there was something about the whole *setup*—

and when it came time for the sentimental bitter statement, well, instead, this big guy Kesey dragged a piano out of his house and they all set about axing the hell out of it and burning it up, calling it "the oldest living thing on Perry Lane," only they were giggling and yahooing about it,

high as coons, in some weird way, all of them, hard-grabbing off the stars, and it was hard as hell to make the End of an Era story come out right in the papers, with nothing but this kind of freaking Olsen & Johnson material to work with,

but they managed to go back with the story they came with, End of an Era, the cliché intact, if they could only blot out the cries in their ears of *Ve-ni-son Chi-li*— [p. 48]

Wolfe returns to this theme in the last chapter of the book, when he shows television reporters completely missing the truth of the "Acid Graduation" in their obtrusive attempt to find the story they have come expecting to find: "The TV crews are trying to edge up close and jockey for position. Is this where he tells the kids to turn off LSD? . . . Which is what—we came for . . . *Waves?*" (p. 353). Whereas Kesey fails to communicate because he abandons form and opens his movie to all experience, the mass media fail because they impose formulas and close themselves off from experience.

Wolfe presents his own role as new journalist as an alternative to both errors. Portraying his initial involvement in the subject as a comic example of the conventional journalist's attempt to bring a preconceived story to an experience he does not know or understand, he tells us that he first had "the idea of going to Mexico and trying to find Kesey and do a story on Young Novelist Real-Life Fugitive" (p. 5). But he was still trying to find out where Kesey was in Mexico when he was captured in California. Wolfe's description of his first meeting with Kesey in jail is a symbolic parody of the barrier between his preconceived story and Kesey's experience. As they stand in separate isolation booths and talk over a static-filled telephone hook-up, Wolfe asks about Kesey's fugitive days in Mexico: "That was still the name of my story, Young Novelist Fugitive Eight Months in Mexico" (p. 7). Wolfe "can see his lips moving two feet away," but the voice "crackles over the telephone like it was coming from Brisbane" (p. 7). Wolfe is "scribbling like mad" (p. 7) as Kesey begins providing information. Wolfe makes a point of telling the reader that "well, to be frank, I didn't know what in the hell it was all about" (p. 7). The separate glass booths and static-filled telephone represent the barriers between two subjective realities, barriers that contrived and distorting communications media cannot bridge. Wolfe's comic self-portrayal signals his recognition of this problem.

Unlike conventional journalists, Wolfe shows himself as a fallible person who is nevertheless willing to learn. He gradually abandons his preconceived story and devotes his full time to not only observing but also experiencing the subject: "Despite the skepticism I brought here, *I* am suddenly experiencing *their* feeling. I am sure of it. I feel like I am in on something the outside world, the world I came from, could not possibly comprehend . . ." (p. 25). Wolfe, of course, never completely abandons that skepticism, and his account of Kesey's quest is as intellectually outside as it is experientially inside the protagonist's "fantasy"; it both reports and shapes. *The Electric Kool-Aid Acid Test* has validity precisely because it refuses to settle for either the unselective subjectivity of Kesey's movie or the rigid objectivity of the mass media's clichés. By combining exhaustive research with an experimental willingness to use and violate the formal conventions of journalism and of the novel, Wolfe creates a work which recounts factual events while conveying the subjective realities of his characters. And from his use of unusual punctuation to his allusions to Poe's "A Descent into the Maelstrom," Wolfe insistently brings his subject within his personal vision, frankly interpreting extreme experience for his reader. Far from being the "realist" he calls himself, Wolfe is an assertively self-reflexive experimentalist who, through pattern and style, transforms as he reports, responds as he represents.

6

Memory, Fragments and "Clean Information": Michael Herr's *Dispatches*

Some people found it distasteful or confusing if I told them that, whatever else, I'd loved it there too. And if they just asked, "What was your scene there?" I wouldn't know what to say either, so I'd say I was trying to write about it and didn't want to dissipate it. But before you could dissipate it you had to locate it, Plant you now, dig you later: information printed on the eye, stored in the brain, coded over skin and transmitted by blood, maybe what they meant by "blood consciousness." And transmitted over and over without letup on increasingly powerful frequencies until you either received it or blocked it out one last time, informational Death of a Thousand Cuts, each cut so precise and subtle you don't even feel them accumulating, you just get up one morning and your ass falls off.

—*Dispatches*

Beginning in the latter half of 1967, Michael Herr spent two years in Vietnam while on a rather unstructured assignment for *Esquire*. Only twenty-seven years old when he arrived, he witnessed such climactic events as the Tet offensive and the siege of Khe Sahn; his long articles appeared in *Esquire* as well as in *Rolling Stone* and *New American Review*. Over the next eight years he continued writing about his Vietnam experience, blending both the published and unpublished work into a much-revised and worked-over book entitled simply *Dispatches* (1977). The book had been eagerly awaited by readers of Herr's earlier articles, which Francis Ford Coppola acknowledges as an influence on his film *Apocalypse Now* (he later had Herr write the film's narration), and the critical reception seemed to extend almost beyond acclaim to gratitude. In the *Saturday Review*, for instance, William Plummer called it "hands down, *the* book about Americans in Vietnam," [1] and *Newsweek*'s Peter Prescott said that it "may be the best book any American has written about any war." [2] Such praise, while appropriate to the considerable quality of the book, reflects in its extravagance American readers' need for a work that would help them comprehend the war, the media event most responsible for the unreality of American experience in the 1960's.

For Americans at home, the Vietnam war differed from previous ones in at least two crucial ways. It was a media war, highly visible in the morning papers and on the evening news; paradoxically, it was an unreal war, characterized by recurring images of destruction, power, and speed in place of any visible enemy, geographical objectives, or lines of conflict. Conventional journalism brought innumerable facts about the war into American homes. But, as Herr comments in *Dispatches*, because of the rigid conventions of "objectivity" within which the media worked, "it would be as impossible to know what Vietnam looked like from reading most newspaper stories as it would be to know how it smelled." [3] Because realistic fiction's weak author-reader contract required an emphasis on the "plausible," it was also unable to convey the hallucinatory ambience of such a war. In contrast, new journalism afforded a writer peculiar means for surmounting these difficulties. With the combination of a first-person journalistic contract and innovative fictional techniques, Herr was free to develop a form that would present the actual experience of the Vietnam conflict, while also offering a way to meaningfully explore its significance.

As one reads *Dispatches*, the advantages of new journalism as a literary strategy for dealing with the Vietnam war become quickly apparent. Rather than merely reporting and thus exacerbating strange facts, or laboring over the construction of a credible fictional representation of an inherently incredible actuality, Herr is able to engage his subject directly and innovatively. In *Dispatches* Herr avoids the need to restrict himself to the plausible world of the realistic novelist by working from a journalistic contract, and he makes the objective goals of the conventional journalist irrelevant by constructing his book not as a direct report on the Vietnam war, but as an exploration of his *memory* of the war. *Dispatches* consists of a series of fragments, ranging from the briefest snapshots to fully dramatized episodes, arranged in nonchronological order. These fragments are subsumed within the larger structure of Herr's meditating consciousness as he probes for the essential meaning of his Vietnam experience. A metafiction, *Dispatches* is self-reflexively presented as the journey of its author through his own consciousness. He repetitiously journeys from innocence to experience in these fragmentary memories, searching for a truth that will be sufficiently central to the experience. In texture and form Herr's book is thus closely related to, and perhaps influenced by, the fabulist experiments of such writers as Kosinski and Barthelme, who also rely on ironic memory and juxtaposed fragments. By applying similar methods and strategies to his journalistic material, Herr is able to avoid the limitations of realistic fiction and conventional journalism. Instead of concentrating on surfaces, he constructs a self-reflexive fable—a highly stylized and emblematic exploration of the images that reside in his consciousness long after the actual events have passed. In this way Herr makes the necessity of exploring and ordering the events in Vietnam, not the events themselves, his true subject. Like the work of the other new journalists studied in this book, *Dispatches* possesses the special power of a factual contract but is, in its form and concerns, a work of the new fiction as much as is any work of fabulation.

"Information" is a term that regularly occurs in *Dispatches*. The variety of contexts in which it appears ironically emphasizes Herr's intense search for more than the superficial "facts" gathered by the mass media. Starting with the fragmentary facts of his own experience, he seeks as a self-conscious writer to shape a form that will afford some understanding of them. Herr's book is assertively about its own language and form, for Herr knows the difficulty of communicating extreme experience in a way that is both accurate and meaningful. This goal came to embody a moral imperative for him. One of the most memorable (if perhaps somewhat overly dramatized) scenes in *Dispatches* portrays a battle-shocked marine getting off a helicopter and saying to Herr, "Okay, man, you go on, you go on out of here you

cocksucker, but I mean it, you tell it! You tell it, man. If you don't
tell it . . ." (p. 207). Having come face to face with the war and
having developed an obligation to the participants to "tell it,"
Herr is acutely aware that his tool—language—was generally
used during the war as, at best, a cosmetic. In one of many
passages excoriating this disinformation, he speaks of how

nothing so horrible ever happened upcountry that it was beyond language fix and press relations, a squeeze fit into the computers would
make the heaviest numbers jump up and dance. . . . Those men called
dead Vietnamese "believers," a lost American platoon was "a black
eye," they talked as though killing a man was nothing more than
depriving him of his vigor. [p. 42]

Herr perceives, in such terminology, the dangers of language
and form in constructing his own book. Beyond the calculated
euphemisms and statistical mirages employed by American offi-
cials, he sees a deeper gulf between the consciousness of
Americans and the actuality of the war that from the beginning
produced an artificial, fictive "reality" conditioning the nature
and course of the experience. The importance of this theme is
established by his opening *Dispatches* with a description of his
meditations while viewing an old map of Vietnam on the wall of
his Saigon apartment. He is fascinated by the map's complete
lack of relation to the contemporary Vietnam ("That map was a
marvel, especially now that it wasn't real anymore") and by how
useless any map now was in understanding the reality of the
Vietnam landscape:

It was late '67 now, even the most detailed maps didn't reveal much
anymore; reading them was like trying to read the faces of the Vietnamese, and that was like trying to read the wind. We knew that the
uses of most information were flexible, different pieces of ground told
different stories to different people. We also knew that for years now
there had been no country here but the war. [p. 3]

The relationship of a map to a territory is of course a common
semantic analogy for that of language to reality, and Herr's
opening use of the map suggests not only the literal alteration of
the landscape by American technology but also the self-deceiving
alteration of that destructive reality by a deceptive language.

Dispatches is permeated by examples of the gulf between

official language and actuality, and they call special attention to Herr's own language. The fragmented, intensely egocentric structure of the book also ensures that Herr's prose remains in the foreground, relatively free from the competing claims on the reader's attention of narrative line and sustained characterization. Like so many fabulist works, *Dispatches* presents itself to the reader as words. But in this book words are chosen in an arduous attempt to capture the quality of actual experience, without recourse to the stock language provided by a culture that is ever ready to tame experience by transmitting it in familiar formulas.

This consistent search for the accurate linguistic construction of the quality of an actual experience is what unites the apparently contradictory aspects of Herr's prose. To achieve his goal, Herr knew that neither objective reporting of external facts nor subjective reliance on an outpouring of emotion would be enough. He indicates the inadequacy of reporting by explaining his youthful reaction to *Life* magazine photographs of atrocities:

Even when the picture was sharp and clearly defined, something wasn't clear at all, something repressed that monitored the images and withheld their essential information. . . . I could have looked until my lamps went out and I still wouldn't have accepted the connection between a detached leg and the rest of my body, or the poses and positions that always happened (one day I'd hear it called "response-to-impact"), bodies wrenched too fast and violently into unbelievable contortion. [p. 18]

Herr goes on to say that, even when he experienced such scenes at first-hand in Vietnam, he had the same reaction: he was unable to comprehend the actuality before him, as his consciousness seemed to protect him from the reality of the experience. Herr knows that, if he is to capture the reality, he must then go beyond reporting, for the struggle is as much with his and the reader's consciousness as it is with the facts.

Herr also sees the expression of immediate emotion as inadequate to the experience: "Coming back, telling stories, I'd say, 'Oh man I was scared,' and, 'Oh God I thought it was all over,' a long time before I knew how scared I was really supposed to be, or how clear and closed and beyond control 'all over' could become" (p. 21). Herr's recognition of the inadequacy of his perception and language during and immediately after the experience is the basis of his style—indeed, of the book's plan.

First, it is behind his presentation of experience through the mode of memory. One of the great strengths of *Dispatches* is its extraordinary vividness. Herr achieves that vividness not by presenting immediate experience, but through an intensely felt act of shaping memory. He writes in the past tense, begins the book with a long section entitled "Breathing In," written from a perspective well after his stay in Vietnam, and ends in "Breathing Out," telling about how he returned to the United States having only "performed half an act" (p. 251). Only when the distancing of time allows him to probe and order experience through memory and art can he complete the act of going to Vietnam. By making the experience meaningful (for that matter, even real) through the ordering process of reflection, his experience gradually acquires the rich shape and texture of controlled fable.

As a result, Herr constructs each of his fragments as a clearly shaped and assertively lesson-giving parable. In one particularly memorable but typical passage Herr reconstructs with extraordinary intensity the fear he felt during combat:

But once it was actually going on, things were different. You were just like everyone else, you could no more blink than spit. It came back the same way every time, dreaded and welcome, balls and bowels turning over together, your senses working like strobes, free-falling all the way down to the essences and then flying out again in a rush to focus, like the first strong twinge of tripping after an infusion of psilocybin, reaching in at the point of calm and springing all the joy and all the dread ever known, *ever* known by *everyone* who *ever* lived, unutterable in its speeding brilliance, touching all the edges and then passing, as though it had all been controlled from outside, by a god or by the moon. [p. 135]

This passage—with its clipped words; violent images of ascent and descent, expansion and contraction; rhythmic embodiment of total abandon and complete control—brilliantly conveys an extreme experience. But it moves beyond expression to an alteration of perception when Herr concludes it by drawing the clear point of a parable while shocking the reader's conventional expectations:

And every time, you were so weary afterward, so empty of everything but being alive that you couldn't recall any of it, except to know that it was like something else you had felt once before. It remained obscure for a long time, but after enough times the memory took shape and substance and finally revealed itself one afternoon during the breaking off of a firefight. It was the feeling you'd had when you were much, much younger and undressing a girl for the first time. [pp. 135–36]

This conclusion works not only through shock, but also through the reader's sudden recognition of the actual rightness of it—for Herr's preceding reconstruction of the experience of combat has been in terms of sexual excitement, though it has only now, after a long process of ordering reflection, been so named. Herr thus asserts that the information comes as much from the act of shaping memory and art as from the original experience.

More completely than in either Mailer's or Thompson's journalistic works, works to which I think Herr clearly owes a debt, *Dispatches* is centered in the consciousness of the author. Yet it is much less likely to be considered a chapter of an autobiography, for Herr tells us almost nothing of his past, nor does he tell us anything of his appearance or character not intrinsically related to the experience he is reporting at that moment. Rather than displaying the author-hero foregrounded against a historical event, as in *The Armies of the Night* and *Fear and Loathing: On the Campaign Trail '72*, we have in *Dispatches* a form and style embodying a virtually complete merger of authorial consciousness with experience. Herr makes his consciousness (and thus his language) the substance of the book, because he perceives it to be the only reality he can give to the war. That is, as I have suggested, the major truth he seems to have brought back from Vietnam: having experience, acquiring new facts, is not in itself the same as acquiring new information. One must also relive that experience through memory and art, shaping the facts into a personally constructed form that will embody a meaning not available in the fictive forms already imposed upon the experiencing mind by one's culture.

To convey the quality of his experience and yet seek to comprehend it, Herr portrays Vietnam through a fragmentary structure united only by a perceiving, meditating consciousness. Since he

traveled about Vietnam without restriction as long as helicopters
or other means of transportation were available, this structure
correlates with his actual experience. Herr early indicates the
plan of the book by describing his experience of the war:

As a technique for staying alive it [mobility] seemed to make as much
sense as anything, given naturally that you were there to begin with and
wanted to see it close; it started out sound and straight but it formed a
cone as it progressed, because the more you moved the more you saw,
the more you saw the more besides death and mutilation you risked,
and the more you risked of that the more you would have to let go of
one day as a "survivor." Some of us moved around the war like crazy
people until we couldn't see which way the run was even taking us
anymore, only the war all over its surface with occasional, unexpected
penetration. [p. 8]

Herr's method for communicating that experience and achieving
"penetration" or insight was to empathize so completely with
any and all the situations and characters that he could gain
understanding relatively undistorted by personal attitudes or
preconceptions. This process, he says, took over a year, by which
time he "felt so plugged in to all the stories and the images and the
fear that even the dead started telling me stories, you'd hear them
out of a remote but accessible space where there were no ideas,
no emotions, no facts, no proper language, only clean information" (p. 31). There were dangers in this. Herr tells of how the
war overwhelmed him with information: he "went to cover the
war and the war covered me" (p. 20). But at the same time he
found that "a lot of things had to be unlearned before you could
learn anything at all" (p. 210). He had to strip his consciousness
of prepackaged images and ideas assimilated from "Television
City" before he could understand the actual experience, see it
and not a media-supplied fiction of his culture. As a result, Herr's
consciousness—while the essential reality of every word in *Dispatches*—lacks the philosophical substance of Mailer's persona
or the sharp outline of Thompson's. Instead, as one of the meanings of the title of Herr's opening chapter, "Breathing In," suggests, he seeks in *Dispatches* to sort out through memory and art
the actual shape of his experience, so that his book will become a
map dynamic and accurate enough to serve as a guide to the

mysterious territory of the war's reality. This analogy is indicated not only by the opening passage referred to earlier, and by a second map—the American military's arbitrary division and naming of Vietnam into convenient but unreal quadrants—somewhat later (p. 92), but also by a map he mentions in the final chapter, "Breathing Out." He carried with him in Vietnam a *National Geographic* map of Indochina, marking it with pencil dots and crosses to indicate where he had been near or in combat. Since he took it back to the United States, he is able to use it as a suggestive image of the process of the war experience being ordered by his remembering consciousness: "Real places, then real only in the distance behind me, faces and places sustaining serious dislocation, mind slip and memory play. When the map fell apart along the fold lines its spirit held together, it landed in safe but shaky hands . . ." (p. 255).

To communicate the ordering act of his mind, Herr organizes the nervous, disorienting juxtaposition of scenes, brief narratives, and longer tales within a pattern of a recurring journey from innocence to experience. Such a journey is to be expected in war literature, but by structuring it repetitively in scene after scene, Herr causes the reader to participate in it primarily as Herr's act of memory and of art, a mental journey necessarily taken again and again after an actual experience as he seeks to find its true shape. Herr avoids presenting his passage from innocence to experience in a conventional narrative structure representing a single climactic experience; instead, he constructs a series of fragments representing his mind's probing for a true comprehension of experiences already undergone but not properly assimilated and patterned.

Our initial glimpses of Herr's own entry into the war experience are, while extraordinarily vivid, predictable enough. We participate in the shock of his first contact with troops just returned from combat, when he walked through an airport runway of troops, "a thousand men on a cold rainy airfield after too much of something I'd never really know, 'a way you'll never be,' dirt and blood and torn fatigues, eyes that poured out a steady charge of wasted horror" (p. 22). Immersing us in these sights and sounds and smells of war, he emphasizes his ridiculous innocence in his new role of "war correspondent" by reporting that he heard a radio playing "Sam the Sham singing, 'Lil' Red Riding Hood, I don't think little big girls should, Go walking in these spooky old woods alone. . . .' " (p. 22). Such an initiation into the reality of war as terror, while powerfully portrayed, is one that our classic writers have taught us to expect.

Ordering the book through the mode of memory, Herr replays this pattern of discovery of unexpected horror in other experiences. The reader's focus gradually shifts from the originally experiencing consciousness to the authorial one which is obsessively coming back to them. In one scene, for instance, he tells of his gratefully wearing a helmet tossed to him, before later discarding it when he realized it must have belonged to a dead grunt. And his long narrative about Khe Sahn ends with his subsequent discovery, in casual conversation, that a Marine he had befriended was later killed. In another scene he remembers how a hysterical helicopter pilot forced him to cover the face of a corpse. In yet another, reminiscent of the scene in *Catch-22* when Yossarian witnesses Snowden's spilling entrails, he re-creates his shocked observation of a spreading dark spot on a soldier's uniform as he rides with him in a helicopter. A recurrent point made by the authorial consciousness is that these events never really penetrated his innocence at the time; since, in his experiencing consciousness, they had precedent only in film and literature, they were never quite real to him. (This theme has been most famously developed in Hemingway's "Indian Camp." After witnessing violent suffering and death, Nick, protected by his youthful innocence, is ironically shown leaving the experience, "sure he would never die.") Reporting his reaction to the "dark spot" on the soldier, Herr echoes this theme with his own ironic assertion that "he was dead, but not (I knew) really dead" (p. 168). This perception could only be achieved after the experience, through the intense probing and reflection of a consciousness determined to use memory to reexplore it.

As in the previous great American war books—*The Red Badge of Courage, A Farewell to Arms, Catch-22*—a secret is being held back in *Dispatches*. The revelations of the earlier books, as suggested above, are echoed throughout *Dispatches*; after all, Herr knows that the discovery of war as horror, as trap, as absurdity can no longer be truly new for a reader, or even for a participant. If Herr only re-created these experiences in the context of the Vietnam war, *Dispatches* would lack the originality (and thus the power) of its predecessors. But by constructing his work as a dramatization of his remembering consciousness, probing and searching for the true meaning of his experience, Herr has from the beginning been leading us toward the "heart of darkness" he finally came to see. As he says, "All right, yes, it had been a groove being a war correspondent, hanging out with the grunts and getting close to the war, touching it, losing yourself in it and trying yourself against it" (p. 206). The great writers of realism and modernism broke through the clichés of their culture to bring the news that war was not a romantic playing field of heroes, but a hell. Herr, who as a new journalist looks directly at external facts and at himself, brings back the news that war *is* hell—but an all-too-attractive playing ground for fantasizing heroes nevertheless. That may be the final, most awful discovery of his experience. Nevertheless, it suggests that an understanding of the national experience involves a similar discovery about the cultural forms of the national consciousness.

Herr's self-reflexive exploration of his consciousness as it struggles to move beyond the innocence of its preformulated structures appears as an emblem of the national consciousness's difficult journey toward self-discovery in Vietnam. He knows, for instance, that he and his fellow correspondents tended to comprehend combat as television melodrama. He comically reveals that tendency when he tells how he began laughing, while he ran from position to position under fire during Tet, as he realized he had just asked a Marine to "cover" him and a colleague—a phrase he realizes he must have learned from combat *movies*, rather than from combat *experience*. But the comedy ends when Herr shows the reality that intrudes upon his private melodrama. He stops laughing when he sees the corpse of a young girl lying in the street, her bare feet being approached by flames. Herr presents his personal difficulty in not overlaying the senseless death of war with melodramatic ritual as a parable of an affliction universal for a nation fed on video fantasies.

Earlier in the book, speaking of Americans in Vietnam (including draftees and war correspondents), Herr comments that "somewhere all the mythic tracks intersected, from the lowest

John Wayne wetdream to the most aggravated soldier-poet fantasy, and where they did I believe that everyone knew everything about everyone else, every one of us there a true volunteer" (p. 20). Soldiers were "wiped out by seventeen years of war movies before coming to Vietnam to get wiped out for good," for he saw them "actually making war movies in their heads, doing little guts-and-glory Leatherneck tap dances under fire, getting their pimples shot off for the networks" when they were in combat in the presence of a television crew (p. 209). He sees a similar innocence behind the melodramatic gestures dominating Marine strategy, most starkly portrayed in his Kafkaesque chapter on Khe Sahn, where the Marine leadership refused to have its troops "dig in." In the largest terms, he suggests that a similar innocence lies behind the entire American perception of its mission and methods in Vietnam, consistently expressed in terms of the stock wisdom of past wars with the Indians or the Nazis, even more particularly in terms of our mythic versions of those wars. His perception of this power of the national consciousness to create illusory "facts" out of mental visions is emphasized by his speculation that America's entry into the Vietnam war could be dated from the time when our ancestors "found the New England woods too raw and empty for their peace and filled them up with their own imported devils" (p. 49). Herr's point is that, for individuals and for the nation, the previously formulated structures supplied by our culture prevented us from at first perceiving the reality of the Vietnam war, often even after experiencing it first-hand. The epistemological implication is that even the most terrible facts will not provide sufficient information for one to grasp truth, unless the structures of consciousness organizing those facts are changed as well.

Perhaps this realization is afforded to Herr, even forced upon him, by his intensely self-conscious new journalistic form. Since he is his own most central subject, Herr has the problem and opportunity of admitting complete complicity in the war. Echoing yet another American classic of self-discovery, *Huckleberry Finn*, he says that he came to war believing that he had "to be able to look at anything," but he soon found that "you were as responsible for everything you saw as you were for everything you did" (p. 20). Herr's factual and mental journey provides us with the information he found while in Vietnam and, even more crucially, while writing his book. Like those from the mass media, he went to Vietnam to gather facts. But unlike them (or at least unlike the corporate structures for which they were finally only providing raw data), Herr was not satisfied to formulate those facts into previously provided structures, not even those structures available to him from previous war literature. Instead, he insisted on keeping his mind open to the experiences he was actually having, and developing a literary form that would communicate them. He finally created an intensely self-reflexive work in which the act of writing as much as that of traveling forms a fable of self-discovery. By so ordering a work of reportage, of "nonfiction," Herr has contributed to our comprehension of the Vietnam war as, in part, a product of the American consciousness. He has also affirmed the power of a new journalism that is a genre of the new fiction.

Epilogue

Fiction is the literary form most concerned with interior consciousness, while journalism is that most concerned with public fact. New journalism attempts to deal with a world in which the latter has, at an unassimilable pace, entered the former. Each of the new journalists whose works I have discussed attempts to provide the reader with facts, but more importantly with patterns. As diverse as they may be in forms and themes, Mailer's *Armies of the Night*, *Of a Fire on the Moon*, and *The Executioner's Song*, Thompson's *Fear and Loathing in Las Vegas* and *Fear and Loathing: On the Campaign Trail '72*, Wolfe's *Electric Kool-Aid Acid Test*, and Herr's *Dispatches* are all embodiments of human consciousnesses directly confronting the actual world—making it into a fictive world possessing shape and significance. We live in a society where actual people and events are daily experienced as images in the mass media. New journalists directly confront the actualities behind these images and interpret them for us, fulfilling the function of explorers who pass through the frontiers of ordinary experience and then return to tell us what is on the other side.

In new journalistic works, authors draw readers into self-consciously fictive orderings of factual experience so that they can experience them as significant realities. New journalists portray the strange phenomena of contemporary "reality" as both actual and meaningful—though tentatively so, since the patterned experiences provided are presented as clearly fictive (which is to say human) constructs. These works thus function as fables, with the added impact of fact. Readers and critics, however, have often doubted the factual validity of any literature so resolutely fictive in form. I have tried to deal with this issue in my consideration of the works, pointing out the exact nature of the journalistic contracts involved, their relative strengths and weaknesses, and the technical methods by which the authors apply them. I have tried to show that the nature of the contracts of *The*

Armies of the Night and *The Electric Kool-Aid Acid Test* are essential to their formal success, since the ability to draw the reader into an experience of these works as fact is intrinsic to their aesthetic plans.

But the journalistic contracts are primarily means to an end. The end is that of all serious fiction and most especially of fabulist fiction: the perceiving and creating of patterns by which the individual can meaningfully experience his world. The authors considered here have turned the shaping power of imagination upon journalistic subjects because such material has become a crucial part of daily human experience. But the "news" each brings pertains less to facts than to how those facts relate to one another. Ultimately, the news is of the efficacy and necessity of patterning itself.

These patterns, like all human knowledge, originate in the consciousness of the artist-reporter as much as in the actuality. Mailer found that the moon flight mirrored his perception of life as a Manichean struggle; Thompson found his nightmares of human bestiality fulfilled in the presidential campaign; Wolfe found the explanation for the Merry Pranksters in his favorite sociological theories; Herr found himself experiencing combat in terms of fantasies he had acquired from television. The patterns of these new journalistic works also originate in the collective consciousness embodied in the culture which has produced the authors. *Of a Fire on the Moon* is presented as a struggle to write a great book, to find a literary theme and form equal to the subject. *Fear and Loathing: On the Campaign Trail '72* parodies both the innocent's journey through experience and the composition of a great work. *The Electric Kool-Aid Acid Test* views its climactic events through the lenses of a classic American short story. *Dispatches* alludes both explicitly and implicitly to classic American war literature. Such highly stylized and allusive patterns draw attention to themselves *as patterns*; they function clearly as thematic overlays, products of an interpretive consciousness standing outside factual events.

Yet the new journalists also derive their power from convincingly demonstrating that the thematic patterns of their works are inherent in the material as well, that they themselves are constructing forms only to reveal actual ones. The power of new journalism lies in this relationship between the fictive nature of its created form and the factual nature of its content. The works considered in this study succeed as new journalism partly because of their dynamic balance between fiction and journalism, between the forming power of a consciousness and the impervious force of actual events.

Notes

1

1. Nicolaus Mills, "Introduction," in *The New Journalism*, ed. Nicolaus Mills (New York: McGraw-Hill, 1974), p. xvii.

2. Gay Talese, *Fame and Obscurity* (New York: World, 1970), p. vii.

3. Michael L. Johnson, *The New Journalism* (Lawrence: Univ. Press of Kansas, 1971), p. 80.

4. "Catcher in the Wry," *Newsweek*, 1 May 1972, p. 65. Similarly, Harold Hayes has indicated that some minor deletions were made in Wolfe's first new journalistic manuscript because "they bore too marked a similarity to the voice of Holden Caulfield in *Catcher in the Rye.*" See Harold Hayes, "Editor's Notes on the New Journalism," *Esquire*, Jan. 1972, rpt. in *The Reporter As Artist*, ed. Ronald Weber (New York: Hastings House, 1974), p. 261.

5. Walter Lippmann, "Stereotypes," in *Public Opinion* (1922), rpt. in *Mass Media and Communication*, ed. Charles S. Steinberg (New York: Hastings House, 1972), pp. 112–20.

6. Timothy Crouse, *The Boys on the Bus* (1972; rpt. New York: Ballantine, 1974).

7. Edward Jay Epstein, *News from Nowhere* (1973; rpt. New York: Vintage, 1974), p. 180.

8. Alexander Cockburn, "Press Clips," *National Village Voice*, 20 Sept. 1976, p. 21.

9. Daniel Boorstin, *The Image or What Happened to the American Dream* (New York: Atheneum, 1961).

10. "The Tedium Is the Message," *Time*, 19 July 1976, p. 53.

11. Tom Wolfe, *The Kandy-Kolored Tangerine-Flake Streamline Baby* (1965; rpt. New York: Pocket Books, 1966), p. xii.

12. *Ibid.*, pp. xiii–xiv.

13. Norman Mailer, *The Armies of the Night* (1968; rpt. New York: New American Library, 1968), p. 14.

14. *Ibid.*, p. 245.

15. Michael Herr, *Dispatches* (New York: Alfred A. Knopf, 1977), p. 218.

16. *Ibid.*, p. 215.

17. Tom Wolfe, "The New Journalism," in *The New Journalism*, ed. Tom Wolfe and E. W. Johnson (New York: Harper and Row, 1973), p. 34.

18. Philip Roth, "Writing American Fiction," *Commentary*, March 1961, rpt. in *The American Novel Since World War II*, ed. Marcus Klein (Greenwich, Conn.: Fawcett, 1969), p. 144.

19. David Lodge, *The Novelist at the Crossroads* (Ithaca, N.Y.: Cornell Univ. Press, 1971), p. 33.

20. Nathalie Sarraute, *The Age of Suspicion*, trans. Maria Jolas (New York: George Braziller, 1963), p. 63.

21. Zavarzadeh's book (Urbana: Univ. of Illinois Press, 1976) is at its best when discussing the problematic nature of contemporary reality and the problems it presents for the realistic fiction writer. But while he follows Lodge and others in his view of the nonfiction novel and fabulation (he uses the term "transfiction" for the latter) as responses to this crisis, he argues that the former represent attempts to avoid or undercut the transforming function of the imagination and are uniformly absurdist in their intentions. As I stated in the preface, I disagree with this view, though I find many of Zavarzadeh's specific observations about the works illuminating. Hollowell's book (Chapel Hill: Univ. of North Carolina Press, 1977), in contrast, is a survey that, while it also develops the crisis in contemporary reality and views fabulist fiction and new journalism as related responses to it, largely relies on Wolfe's view of the techniques as realistic.

22. Robert J. Van Dellen, "We've Been Had by the New Journalism: A Put Down," in *New Journalism*, ed. Marshall Fishwick (Bowling Green, Ohio: Bowling Green Univ. Popular Press, 1975), p. 128.

23. Wilfrid Sheed, "A Fun-House Mirror," *New York Times Book Review*, 3 Dec. 1972, rpt. in Weber, ed., *The Reporter As Artist*, p. 295.

24. Dwight Macdonald, "Parajournalism, or Tom Wolfe and His Magic Writing Machine," *New York Review of Books*, 26 Aug. 1965, rpt. in Weber, ed., *The Reporter As Artist*, p. 227.

25. For an excellent study of these characteristics as found in contemporary fiction of this era, see Robert Scholes, *Fabulation and Metafiction* (Urbana: Univ. of Illinois Press, 1979), an expanded version of his seminal *The Fabulators* (New York: Oxford Univ. Press, 1967).

26. Thomas Griffith, "Fear and Loathing and Ripping Off," *Time*, 19 July 1976, p. 53.

27. Wayne C. Booth, "Loathing and Ignorance on the Campaign Trail: 1972," *Columbia Journalism Review* 12, no. 4 (1973): 8.

28. "John Barth: An Interview," *Wisconsin Studies in Contemporary Literature* 6 (1965): 8.

29. One of the most perceptive considerations of these works confusing history and fable is Barbara Foley's "From *U.S.A.* to *Ragtime*: Notes on the Forms of Historical Consciousness in Modern Fiction," *American Literature* 50 (1978): 85–105.

30. "Playboy Interview: Anthony Burgess," *Playboy*, Sept. 1974, p. 76.

31. Northrop Frye, *Anatomy of Criticism* (1957; rpt. Princeton: Princeton Univ. Press, 1971), p. 303.

32. Robert Scholes, *Elements of Fiction* (New York: Oxford Univ. Press, 1968), pp. 1–2.

33. Ernest Hemingway, "Monologue to the Maestro: A High Seas Letter," *Esquire*, Oct. 1935, p. 21.

2

1. Regarding *The Electric Kool-Aid Acid Test*, Wolfe said that he had "been held back by the question of technique" until he began "writing scene by scene where I had the material, but going into straight exposition where that came more naturally" (Tom Wolfe, "The Author's Story," *New York Times Book Review*, 22 July 1973, p. 41). He has made the following similar comments concerning *The Right Stuff*: "I simply had to lay it down, tell the story. I couldn't even use scene-by-scene techniques" (Henry Allen, "The Pyrotechnic Iconoclast, Still Passing the Acid Test," *Washington Post*, 4 Sept. 1979, sec. B, p. 4, col. 1). "I relaxed and said I would use these 'new journalistic' devices where I felt they were right and go to more conventional forms—the essay, for example—where they felt right" (Mort Sheinman, "Zoom! Boom! Voom! Tom Wolfe Blasts Off," *W*, 31 Aug.–7 Sept. 1979, p. 2, col. 3).

2. Barbara Foley, "Fact, Fiction, and 'Reality,' " *Contemporary Literature* 20 (1979): 389–99.

3. "The employment of narrative techniques gives New Journalistic copy a fictional texture rather than a fictual tension. Like history, biography, or the fact novel, the piece is a mono-referential narrative and thus is diametrically different from the nonfiction novel" (*Mythopoeic Reality*, p. 64). Zavarzadeh seems to be saying that the new journalism remains at the factual pole of writing, lacking real fictional coherence. There is no precedent, however, for using the terms "new journalism" and "nonfiction novel" in this way. This distinction becomes particularly confusing when he includes a chapter on Tom Wolfe, often referred to as the "Dean of the New Journalism," as a nonfiction novelist.

4. *Ibid.*, p. 41.

5. Frye, *Anatomy of Criticism*, pp. 73–74.

6. *Ibid.*, p. 303.

7. Norman Mailer, *Some Honorable Men: Political Conventions 1960–1972* (Boston: Little, Brown, 1976), p. xi.

8. Zavarzadeh, *Mythopoeic Reality*, pp. 80–89.

9. *Ibid.*, p. 83.

10. René Wellek and Austin Warren, *Theory of Literature*, 3rd ed. (1942; rpt. New York: Harcourt, Brace, and World, 1970), p. 214.

11. Zavarzadeh, *Mythopoeic Reality*, p. 80.

12. *Ibid.*, pp. 80–81.

3

1. Norman Mailer, *Advertisements for Myself* (New York: G. P. Putnam's Sons, 1959), p. 199.

2. Mailer, *The Armies of the Night*, p. 152. All subsequent references are within the text.

3. Norman Mailer, *Miami and the Siege of Chicago* (New York: New American Library, 1968), p. 56.

4. Stanley T. Gutman, *Mankind in Barbary* (Hanover, N.H.: University Press of New England, 1975), p. 99.

5. In *The Mythopoeic Reality* Zavarzadeh perceives the presence of what he calls "meta-interpretation" in such passages of *The Armies of the Night*, seeing this as a self-negating approach. But as a metafiction of history *The Armies of the Night* does not deny the validity of fiction-making; rather, it emphasizes its absolute necessity. See Zavarzadeh, *Mythopoeic Reality*, pp. 153–76.

6. Mario Puzo, "Generalissimo Mailer: Hero of His Own Dispatches," *Book World*, 28 April 1968, p. 1.

7. Laura Adams, *Existential Battles* (Athens: Ohio Univ. Press, 1976), p. 7.

8. Appeared originally as "A Fire on the Moon," *Life*, 29 Aug. 1969, pp. 24–40; "The Psychology of Astronauts," *Life*, 14 Nov. 1969, pp. 50–63; "A Dream of the Future's Face," *Life*, 9 Jan. 1970, pp. 57–74.

9. Roger Sale, "Watchman, What of the Night?" *New York Review of Books*, 6 May 1971, p. 13. Sale's response to the book is fairly representative, but the most probing criticism has come from Richard Poirier, who perceives in *Of a Fire on the Moon* "evidence that Mailer's imagination of himself is becoming dangerously rigid and circumscribed, particularly when he indulges in rather simple and fashionable concerns about the future of the imagination in an age of technology"

(*Norman Mailer* [New York: Viking, 1972], p. 160). It is true that *Of a Fire on the Moon* often seems almost claustrophobically limited in its subduing of the Apollo mission to Mailer's mental sphere. Nevertheless, Mailer's aesthetic and stylistic achievement in *Of a Fire on the Moon* transcends the limits of his ideas and personality. As a construct of a consciousness's struggle with a great event, *Of a Fire on the Moon* is a literary experience far greater than its worldview.

10. Alfred Kazin, *Bright Book of Life* (Boston: Little, Brown, 1971), p. 238.

11. Norman Mailer, *Of a Fire on the Moon* (Boston: Little, Brown, 1970), pp. 6–7. All subsequent references are within the text.

12. In this theme *Of a Fire on the Moon* is similar to Henry Adams's contemplation of the dynamo in *The Education of Henry Adams*; Mailer may very well have had this work in mind as a model. Many critics have noted the similarity, but for a developed comparison see Gordon O. Taylor, "Of Adams and Aquarius," *American Literature* 46 (1964): 68–82.

13. Mailer's philosophic ordering or "fiction" of reality involves a unique combination of existential and romantic ideas which he first set forth in *Advertisements for Myself*. Viewing the universe as the Manichean battleground of a dialectic or war between dualities which is engaged on various levels of existence (God-Devil, Individual-Totalitarianism, Hip-Square, Growth-Decay, Health-Cancer), he believes, with the romantics, that all reality is linked, and thus recapitulates itself on microcosmic-macrocosmic planes. In relation to this pervasive dialectic he sees man in a potentially heroic existential situation, for he is free to contribute to one or the other of the Manichean forces. In addition to Poirier's book, two of the finest discussions of Mailer's cosmology can be found in the following: Richard D. Finholt, " 'Otherwise How Explain?' Norman Mailer's New Cosmology," *Modern Fiction Studies* 17 (1971): 375–86; Michael Lennon, "A Radical Bridge: Mailer's Narrative Art" (Ph.D. dissertation, Univ. of Rhode Island, 1975).

14. Mailer, *Of a Fire on the Moon* (1970; rpt. New York: New American Library, 1971), p. 335.

15. See especially *An American Dream* (New York: Dial Press, 1965) for Stephen Rojack's recurring identification of the moon with the "abyss."

16. Norman Mailer, *The Executioner's Song* (Boston: Little, Brown, 1979), p. 1052. All subsequent references are within the text.

17. "Crime and Punishment: Gary Gilmore," *Firing Line*, host William F. Buckley, Jr., broadcast on PBS, 4 Nov. 1979.

18. *Ibid.*

19. *Ibid.*

20. See Phillip K. Tompkins, "In Cold Fact," *Esquire*, June 1966, pp. 125–27, 166–68.

21. See Norman Mailer, *The Presidential Papers* (New York: G. P. Putnam's Sons, 1963), p. 51.

4

1. In the Plimpton interview, for instance, Capote discussed the reactions of literary associates when he told them of his journalistic ideas: "When I first formed my theories concerning the nonfiction novel, many people with whom I discussed the matter were unsympathetic. They felt that what I proposed, a narrative form that employed all the techniques of fictional art but was nevertheless immaculately factual, was little more than a literary solution for fatigued novelists suffering from 'failure of imagination.' Personally, I felt that this attitude represented a 'failure of imagination' on their part" (George Plimpton, "The Story Behind a Nonfiction Novel," *New York Times Book Review*, 16 Jan. 1966, p. 2). In *The Armies of the Night* Mailer tells of his suspicion at Robert Lowell's complimenting him as "the best journalist in America": " 'Well, Cal,' said Mailer, using Lowell's nickname for the first time, 'there are days when I think of myself as being the best writer in America' " (*Armies of the Night*, p. 33).

2. Jerome Klinkowitz and Roy R. Behrens, *The Life of Fiction* (Urbana: Univ. of Illinois Press, 1977), p. 31.

3. The term reportedly comes from a description of Thompson's work by Bill Cardoso, a writer Thompson met in 1968 while covering the Nixon campaign for the *National Observer*. "In an admiring note, sent to Thompson after he had written a tour de force on the Kentucky Derby, Cardoso pronounced Hunter's work 'real Gonzo,' and thus the legend was born" (Robert Sam Anson, "The *Rolling Stone* Saga, Part II," *New Times*, 10 Dec. 1976, p. 24).

4. Hunter S. Thompson, *Fear and Loathing: On the Campaign Trail '72* (San Francisco: Straight Arrow Books, 1973), p. 225. Subsequent references are within the text.

5. Morris Dickstein, "The Working Press, the Literary Culture, and the New Journalism," *Georgia Review* 30 (1976): 860.

6. Kurt Vonnegut, Jr., "A Political Disease," *Harper's*, July 1973, p. 94.

7. Hunter S. Thompson, *Fear and Loathing in Las Vegas* (New

York: Popular Library, 1971), p. 178. Subsequent references are within the text.

8. Anson, "*Rolling Stone* Saga," p. 24. This article is the fullest biographical discussion of Thompson yet published. One problem in acquiring a view of Thompson that penetrates his persona is that writers often seem compelled to participate in this creation; as, for instance, in the biographical portrait which precedes the *Playboy* interview ("*Playboy* Interview: Hunter Thompson," *Playboy*, Nov. 1974, pp. 75–76). A short biography which follows *Fear and Loathing in Las Vegas* (pp. 207–8) is most likely written by Thompson. For a view, other than his own, of Thompson on the campaign trail, see Timothy Crouse's *Boys on the Bus*, especially pp. 328–38. Information on Thompson's youth, including quotations from friends and family, can be found in John Christensen's "On the Trail of the Outlaw Journalist," *Louisville Times Scene*, 22 Jan. 1977, pp. 3, 4, 18. A view of Thompson at home in Woody Creek, Colorado, is provided by Harrison Salisbury in "Travels through America," *Esquire*, Feb. 1976, pp. 43–44. A particularly ambivalent glimpse is presented in Sally Quinn's *We're Going to Make You a Star* (New York: Simon and Schuster, 1975), pp. 155–57.

9. Thompson has carried this adoption of aliases to the point where it represents a parody of schizophrenia. To this day the *Rolling Stone* masthead lists Dr. Hunter S. Thompson under "National Affairs Desk" and Raoul Duke as a contributing editor responsible for "Sports." In his first article after the Watergate scandal began unraveling, Thompson went so far as to present his article as two separate memos placed together by the "Editors": in one, Raoul Duke reported on his communication with Dr. Thompson while the latter recovered in a decompression chamber from an undersea attack by Dr. Kissinger; the other was Dr. Thompson's report from that chamber. All of this is an elaborate parody of the national response to the shock of Watergate. See Raoul Duke, "Memo from the Sports Desk and Rude Notes from a Decompression Chamber in Miami," *Rolling Stone*, 2 Aug. 1973, pp. 8–10.

10. Jonathan Raban, "The New Mongrel," *London Magazine* 13, no. 2 (1973): 100.

11. The "Edge" is a concept with recurring importance in Thompson's work. In *Hell's Angels* he characterizes it as an experience to be attained at the maximum of speed and danger on a motorcycle while still in control, or in a similar psychic situation from drugs. In either case he defines it as "the place of definitions." See Hunter S. Thompson, *Hell's Angels* (New York: Ballantine Books, 1967), p. 344. *Fear and*

Loathing in Las Vegas begins on "the edge of the desert" with the persona moving at a high rate of speed and on drugs. Later, he refers to himself as a "connoisseur of edge-work" (p. 80). In *Campaign Trail* he sees the attractiveness of life on "The Edge" as the chief motivation for participation in a presidential campaign (pp. 495–97). This need to attain "the place of definitions" suggests, perhaps, a reason for his stylistic flattening of events into a private psychic melodrama.

12. Burton Feldman, "Anatomy of Black Humor," *Dissent* 15 (1968), rpt. in Klein, ed., *The American Novel Since World War II*, p. 225.

13. Charles Harris, *Contemporary American Novelists of the Absurd* (New Haven, Conn.: College and Univ. Press, 1971), p. 28.

14. Wolfe and Johnson, eds., *The New Journalism*, p. 172.

15. Thompson seems to have acquired this perception of the American character when observing the reaction of ordinary citizens to the motorcycle gangs. A major theme of *Hell's Angels* is that the general society needs the Hell's Angels or some such menace, and that to a very real extent society elicited its invention by the media.

16. Raney Stanford, "The Return of Trickster: When a Not-a-Hero Is a Hero," *Journal of Popular Culture* 1, no. 3 (1967): 238.

17. Crawford Woods, "The Best Book on the Dope Decade," *New York Times Book Review*, 23 July 1972, p. 17.

18. See Crouse, *The Boys on the Bus*, pp. 328–38.

19. This shift in contract is reflected in the two works' illustrations. The narrative of *Las Vegas* is accompanied by the grotesque sketches of Ralph Steadman; these visual caricatures reinforce the verbal parody. *Campaign Trail*, however, combines Steadman's sketches with photographs. These photographs were clearly selected for their ludicrous qualities, and are usually provided with satirical captions; but, as photographs, they nevertheless emphasize the actuality of the book's subject matter. In fact, *Campaign Trail* is a rare example of a new journalistic work which uses photographs. None of the other books referred to in this study do.

20. Joseph Kanon, "Madness and Filigree," *Saturday Review/Society*, May 1973, p. 76.

21. Booth, "Loathing and Ignorance on the Campaign Trail: 1972," p. 12.

22. Stewart Alsop, "The Clothespin Vote," *Newsweek*, 17 April 1972, p. 108.

23. In addition to this interview, for instance, in which McGovern candidly discussed the Eagleton episode, *Campaign Trail* includes transcripts of a long tape-recording Thompson made of McGovern's

convention strategists explaining the complex methods and motivations with which they purposely lost the South Carolina women's challenge (pp. 289–316).

5

1. For Wolfe's own account of the beginnings of his career, see "The New Journalism," in Wolfe and Johnson, eds., *The New Journalism*, pp. 10–36.

2. Joe David Bellamy, *The New Fiction: Interviews with Innovative American Writers* (Urbana: Univ. of Illinois Press, 1974), p. 86.

3. *Ibid.*, p. 90.

4. Tom Wolfe, *The Electric Kool-Aid Acid Test* (1968; rpt. New York: Bantam Books Inc., 1969), p. 371. All subsequent references are found within the text.

5. Zavarzadeh, *Mythopoeic Reality*, p. 144.

6. "The New Journalism," in Wolfe and Johnson, eds., *The New Journalism*, p. 17.

7. Tom Wolfe, *The Kandy-Kolored Tangerine-Flake Streamline Baby*, pp. 47–48.

8. "The New Journalism," in Wolfe and Johnson, eds., *The New Journalism*, p. 33.

9. Tom Wolfe, "The Author's Story," *New York Times Book Review*, 22 July 1973, p. 41.

10. Bellamy, *New Fiction*, p. 78.

11. Robert D. Jacobs, *Poe: Journalist and Critic* (Baton Rouge: Louisiana State Univ. Press, 1969), pp. 435–36.

12. See Dwight Macdonald, "Parajournalism II: Wolfe and *The New Yorker*," *New York Review of Books*, 3 Feb. 1966, pp. 18–24, and Leonard C. Lewin, "Is Fact Necessary? A Sequel to the *Herald Tribune–New Yorker* Dispute," *Columbia Journalism Review* 4, no. 4 (1966): 29–34.

13. "New Journalism," in Wolfe and Johnson, eds., *The New Journalism*, pp. 23–25. Wolfe sidesteps the issue of his accuracy in these *New Yorker* pieces and instead excludes the pieces from the genre of new journalism altogether: "My article on the *New Yorker* had not even been an example of the new genre; it used neither the reporting techniques nor the literary techniques; underneath a bit of red-flock *Police Gazette* rhetoric, it was a traditional critique, a needle, an attack, an 'essay' of the old school. It had little or nothing to do with anything I had written before." He goes on to denounce his critics' "strategy" in

singling out this "essay" as the particular object of a general assault on new journalism.

14. *Ibid.*, pp. 39–41.

15. The reviews of *The Electric Kool-Aid Acid Test* can be divided into high praise and severe condemnation. Joel Lieber, for instance, saw it as "nonfiction told as experimental fiction; it is a genuine feat and a landmark in reporting style" ("Day-Glo and Light Nights," *Nation*, 23 Sept. 1968, p. 282). But Margot Hentoff viewed the book as the product of a stylistic approach which "divorced from its novelty, revealed its roots as romantic sports columnist newspaperese" ("Dr. Pop," *New York Review of Books*, 22 Aug. 1968, p. 20). Apart from reviews, Wolfe's nonfiction novel has received significant consideration in four books: Michael L. Johnson, *The New Journalism*, pp. 50–64; Tony Tanner, *City of Words* (New York: Harper and Row, 1971), pp. 372–92; Hollowell, *Fact and Fiction*, pp. 126–46; and Zavarzadeh, *Mythopoeic Reality*, pp. 128–53.

16. Wolfe, "The Author's Story," in Wolfe and Johnson, eds., *The New Journalism*, pp. 2, 40–41.

17. Eric W. Carlson, "Introduction," in *Introduction to Poe: A Thematic Reader*, ed. Eric W. Carlson (Glenview, Ill.: Scott, Foresman, 1967), p. xxv.

6

1. William Plummer, "Ecstasy and Death," *Saturday Review*, 7 Jan. 1978, p. 36.

2. Peter S. Prescott, "In the Quagmire," *Newsweek*, 19 June 1978, p. 82.

3. Michael Herr, *Dispatches*, p. 193. Subsequent references are within the text.

Selected Bibliography

ON CONTEMPORARY LITERATURE

This list includes critical work on contemporary fiction, new journalism, or both. Highly selective, it would nevertheless be much longer if it were not for the presence of certain excellent collections, especially those edited by Fishwick and Weber, for I have only rarely listed individual articles that can be found in those works. Anthologies of contemporary fiction or new journalism which include a significant critical or theoretical preface are included.

Ahearn, Marie L. "*The People of the Abyss*: Jack London as New Journalist." *Modern Fiction Studies* 22 (1976): 73–83.

Bellamy, Joe David, ed. *Superfiction, or the American Story Transformed*. New York: Random House, 1975.

Brower, Brock. "Of Nothing But Facts." *American Scholar* 33 (1964): 613–18.

Brown, Charles H. "The Rise of the New Journalism." *Current*, June 1972, pp. 31–38.

Dennis, Everette E., and William L. Rivers. *Other Voices: The New Journalism in America*. San Francisco: Canfield Press, 1974.

Dickstein, Morris. "The Working Press, the Literary Culture, and the New Journalism." *Georgia Review* 30 (1976): 856–77.

Fiedler, Leslie. *The Return of the Vanishing American*. New York: Stein and Day, 1968.

Fishwick, Marshall, ed. *New Journalism*. Bowling Green, Ohio: Bowling Green Univ. Popular Press, 1975.

Flippin, Charles C., ed. *Liberating the Media: The New Journalism*. Washington, D.C.: Acropolis Books, 1974.

Foley, Barbara. "Fact, Fiction, and 'Reality.' " *Contemporary Literature* 20 (1979): 389–99.

————. "From *U.S.A.* to *Ragtime*: Notes on the Forms of Historical Consciousness in Modern Fiction." *American Literature* 50 (1978): 85–105.

French, Michael R. "The American Novel in the Sixties." *Midwest Quarterly* 9 (1968): 365–79.

Friedman, Bruce Jay, ed. *Black Humor*. New York: Bantam, 1965.

Friedman, Melvin J. "The Confessions of Nat Turner: The Convergence of 'Nonfiction Novel' and 'Meditation on History.' " *Journal of Popular Culture* 1 (1967): 166–75.

Graff, Gerald. *Literature Against Itself: Literary Ideas in Modern Society*. Chicago: Univ. of Chicago Press, 1979.

Haack, Dietmar. "Faction: Tendenzen zu einer Kritischen Faktographie in den USA." Pp. 127–46 in *Amerikanische Literatur im 20. Jahrhundert*. Ed. Alfred Weber and Dietmar Haack. Göttingen: Vandenhoeck and Ruprecht, 1971.

Harris, Charles. *Contemporary American Novelists of the Absurd*. New Haven, Conn.: College and Univ. Press, 1971.

Hauck, Richard. *A Cheerful Nihilism: Confidence and "the Absurd" in American Humorous Fiction*. Bloomington: Indiana Univ. Press, 1971.

Heidenry, John. "Yes, Virginia, the Novel Is Not Dead." *Commonweal*, 12 May 1972, pp. 233–37.

Hollowell, John. *Fact and Fiction: The New Journalism and the Nonfiction Novel*. Chapel Hill: Univ. of North Carolina Press, 1977.

Howe, Quincy. "The New Age of the Journalist-Historian." *Saturday Review*, 20 May 1967, pp. 25–27, 69.

Johnson, Michael L. *The New Journalism: The Underground Press, the Artists of Nonfiction, and Changes in the Established Media*. Lawrence: Univ. Press of Kansas, 1971.

Kazin, Alfred. *Bright Book of Life: American Novelists and Storytellers from Hemingway to Mailer*. Boston: Little, Brown, 1971.

————. "Imagination and the Age." *The Reporter*, 5 May 1966, pp. 32–35.

Kennard, Jean E. *Number and Nightmare: Forms of Fantasy in Contemporary Fiction*. Hamden, Conn.: Archon, 1975.

Klein, Marcus, ed. *The American Novel Since World War II*. Greenwich, Conn.: Fawcett, 1969.

Klinkowitz, Jerome. *Literary Disruptions: The Making of a Post-Contemporary American Fiction*. Urbana: Univ. of Illinois Press, 1975.

————, and John Somer, eds. *Innovative Fiction: Stories for the Seventies*. New York: Dell, 1972.

————. *Writing Under Fire: Stories of the Vietnam War*. New York: Dell, 1978.

Krim, Seymour. "An Enemy of the Novel." *Iowa Review* 3 (1972): 60–62.

McCarthy, Mary. "The Fact in Fiction." Pp. 249–70 in *On the Contrary*. New York: Farrar, Straus and Cudahy, 1961.

Mills, Nicolaus, ed. *The New Journalism: A Historical Anthology.*
New York: McGraw-Hill, 1974.

Murphy, James Emmett. "New Journalism in Perspective: Toward an Understanding of the Nonfiction Form." Ph.D. dissertation, Univ. of Iowa, 1973.

Newfield, Jack. "Is There a 'New Journalism'?" *Columbia Journalism Review*, July/Aug. 1972, pp. 45–47.

Newman, Charles. "Beyond Omniscience: Notes toward a Future for the Novel." *TriQuarterly* 10 (1967): 37–52.

Olderman, Raymond M. *Beyond the Waste Land: A Study of the American Novel in the Nineteen-Sixties.* New Haven: Yale Univ. Press, 1972.

Peer, Elizabeth. "New Journalism Now." *Newsweek*, 31 March 1975, p. 67.

————. "Sexy Sociology." *Newsweek*, 21 July 1975, p. 70.

Poirier, Richard. *The Performing Self: Compositions and Decompositions in the Languages of Contemporary Life.* New York: Oxford Univ. Press, 1971.

Prescott, Peter S. "Instant History." *Newsweek*, 3 May 1976, pp. 89–90.

Reston, James, Jr. "Watergate and Non-Fiction Novels." *Chronicle of Higher Education*, 22 Nov. 1976, p. 10.

Scholes, Robert. "Double Perspective on Hysteria." *Saturday Review*, 24 Aug. 1968, p. 37.

————. *The Fabulators.* New York: Oxford Univ. Press, 1967.

————. *Structural Fabulation: An Essay on Fiction of the Future.* Notre Dame, Ind.: Univ. of Notre Dame Press, 1975.

————. *Fabulation and Metafiction.* Urbana: Univ. of Illinois Press, 1979.

Schulz, Max F. *Black Humor Fiction of the Sixties: A Pluralistic Definition of Man and His World.* Athens: Ohio Univ. Press, 1967.

Seelye, John. "The Shotgun behind the Lens." *New Republic*, 11 Aug. 1973, pp. 22–24.

Tanner, Tony. *City of Words: American Fiction 1950–70.* New York: Harper and Row, 1971.

Taylor, Gordon O. "Cast a Cold 'I': Mary McCarthy on Vietnam." *Journal of American Studies* 9 (1975): 103–14.

Weber, Ronald. "Art-Journalism Revisited." *South Atlantic Quarterly* 78 (1979): 275–89.

————, ed. *The Reporter As Artist: A Look at the New Journalism Controversy.* New York: Hastings House, 1974.

White, Hayden. *Metahistory: The Historical Imagination in Nine-teenth-Century Europe*. Baltimore: Johns Hopkins Univ. Press, 1973.

Zavarzadeh, Mas'ud. *The Mythopoeic Reality: The Postwar American Nonfiction Novel*. Urbana: Univ. of Illinois Press, 1976.

THE NEW JOURNALISTS

Primary works are limited to those available in book form and are provided in their order of publication.

Norman Mailer

PRIMARY

The Naked and the Dead. New York: Holt, Rinehart and Winston, 1948.

Barbary Shore. New York: Rinehart and Company, 1951.

The Deer Park. New York: G. P. Putnam's Sons, 1955.

Advertisements for Myself. New York: G. P. Putnam's Sons, 1959.

Deaths for the Ladies (and Other Disasters). New York: G. P. Put-nam's Sons, 1962.

The Presidential Papers. New York: G. P. Putnam's Sons, 1963.

An American Dream. New York: Dial Press, 1965.

Cannibals and Christians. New York: Dial Press, 1966.

The Deer Park: A Play. New York: Dial Press, 1967.

The Short Fiction of Norman Mailer. New York: Dell, 1967.

Why Are We in Vietnam? New York: G. P. Putnam's Sons, 1967.

The Idol and the Octopus: Political Writings of Norman Mailer on the Kennedy and Johnson Administrations. New York: Dell, 1968.

The Armies of the Night: History As a Novel/The Novel As History. New York: New American Library, 1968.

Miami and the Siege of Chicago: An Informal History of the Republi-can and Democratic Conventions of 1968. New York: New Amer-ican Library, 1968.

Of a Fire on the Moon. Boston: Little, Brown, 1970; rpt. New York: New American Library, 1971.

The Prisoner of Sex. Boston: Little, Brown, 1971.

On the Fight of the Century: King of the Hill. New York: Signet, 1971.

Maidstone: A Mystery. New York: New American Library, 1971.

St. George and the Godfather. New York: New American Library, 1972.

Existential Errands. Boston: Little, Brown, 1972.

Marilyn: A Biography. New York: Grosset and Dunlop, 1973.

The Faith of Graffiti. Photographs by Mervin Kurlansky and Jon Naar. Text by Norman Mailer. New York: Praeger, 1974.

The Fight. Boston: Little, Brown, 1975.

Genius and Lust: A Journey Through the Major Writings of Henry Miller. New York: Grove Press, 1976.

Some Honorable Men: Political Conventions 1960–1972. Boston: Little, Brown, 1976.

The Executioner's Song. Boston: Little, Brown, 1979.

SECONDARY

Adams, Laura. *Existential Battles: The Growth of Norman Mailer*. Athens: Ohio Univ. Press, 1976.

_____. *Will the Real Norman Mailer Please Stand Up?* Port Washington, N.Y.: Kennikat Press, 1974.

Behar, Jack. "History and Fiction." *Novel* 3 (1970): 260–65.

Bell, Pearl K. "The Power and the Glory." *New Leader*, 8 Feb. 1971, pp. 16–17.

Berthoff, Warner. "Witness and Testament: Two Contemporary Classics." *New Literary History* 2 (1971): 311–27.

Costa, Peter T. "Norman Mailer: The Novel as Journalism." M.A. thesis, Univ. of California/Berkeley, 1970.

DeMott, Benjamin. "Inside Apollo 11 with Aquarius Mailer." *Saturday Review*, 16 Jan. 1971, pp. 25–27, 57–58.

Finholt, Richard D. " 'Otherwise How Explain?' Norman Mailer's New Cosmology." *Modern Fiction Studies* 17 (1971): 375–86.

Gutman, Stanley T. *Mankind in Barbary: The Individual and Society in the Novels of Norman Mailer*. Hanover, N.H.: Univ. Press of New England, 1975.

Janney, Richard Wayne. "Personnae in Norman Mailer's Autobiographical Reportage." Ph.D. dissertation, Univ. of Delaware, 1975.

Kaufmann, Donald L. "Mailer's Lunar Bits and Pieces." *Modern Fiction Studies* 17 (1971): 451–54.

Leeds, Barry H. *The Structured Vision of Norman Mailer*. New York: New York Univ. Press, 1969.

Lennon, J. Michael. "Mailer's Radical Bridge." *Journal of Narrative Technique* 7 (1977): 170-88.

————. "Mailer's Sarcophagus: The Artist, the Media, and the 'Wad.' " *Modern Fiction Studies* 23 (1977): 179–87.

Lucid, Robert F. "Introduction." In his *The Long Patrol: 20 Years of Writing from the Work of Norman Mailer*. New York: World, 1971.

Merideth, Robert. "The 45-Second Piss: A Left Critique of Norman Mailer and *The Armies of the Night*." *Modern Fiction Studies* 17 (1971): 433–49.

Poirier, Richard. *Norman Mailer*. New York: Viking, 1972.

Radford, Jean. *Norman Mailer: A Critical Study*. New York: Harper and Row, 1975.

Richardson, Jack. "The Aesthetics of Norman Mailer." *New York Review of Books*, 8 May 1969, pp. 3–4.

Sale, Roger. "Watchman, What of the Night?" *New York Review of Books*, 6 May 1971, pp. 13–17.

Schroth, Raymond A. "Mailer on the Moon." *Commonweal*, 7 May 1971, pp. 216–18.

Sisk, John P. "Aquarius Rising." *Commentary*, May 1971, pp. 83–84.

Solotaroff, Robert. *Down Mailer's Way*. Urbana: Univ. of Illinois Press, 1974.

Taylor, Gordon O. "Of Adams and Aquarius." *American Literature* 46 (1974): 68–82.

Werge, Thomas. "An Apocalyptic Voyage: God, Satan, and the American Tradition in Norman Mailer's *Of a Fire on the Moon*." Pp. 108–28 in *America in Change: Reflections on the '60's and '70's*. Ed. Ronald Weber. Notre Dame: Univ. of Notre Dame Press, 1972.

Hunter S. Thompson

PRIMARY

Hell's Angels: A Strange and Terrible Saga. New York: Ballantine Books, 1967.

Fear and Loathing in Las Vegas: A Savage Journey to the Heart of the American Dream. New York: Popular Library, 1971.

Fear and Loathing: On the Campaign Trail '72. San Francisco: Straight Arrow Books, 1973.

The Great Shark Hunt: Strange Tales from a Strange Time. New York: Summit, 1979.

SECONDARY

Anson, Robert Sam. "The *Rolling Stone* Saga: Part II." *New Times*, 10 Dec. 1976, pp. 22–37, 54–61.

Booth, Wayne C. "Loathing and Ignorance on the Campaign Trail: 1972." *Columbia Journalism Review* 12, no. 4 (1973): 7–12.

"Catcher in the Wry." *Newsweek*, 1 May 1972, p. 65.

Christensen, John. "On the Trail of the Outlaw Journalist." *Louisville Times Scene*, 22 Jan. 1977, pp. 3–4, 18.

Crouse, Timothy. *The Boys on the Bus*. New York: Random House, 1972; rpt. New York: Ballantine, 1974, pp. 329–38.

Felton, David. "Hunter Thompson Has Cashed His Check: A Low-Rent Rendezvous with the Doctor of High-Priced Gonzo." *Rolling Stone College Papers*, May/June 1980, pp. 47–51.

Green, James. "Gonzo." Pp. 106–12 in *New Journalism*. Ed. Marshall Fishwick. Bowling Green, Ohio: Bowling Green Univ. Popular Press, 1975.

Griffith, Thomas. "Fear and Loathing and Ripping Off." *Time*, 19 July 1976, pp. 52–53.

Kanon, Joseph. "Madness and Filigree." *Saturday Review/Society*, May 1973, pp. 76, 80.

Klinkowitz, Jerome, and Roy R. Behrens. Pp. 31–43 in *The Life of Fiction*. Urbana: Univ. of Illinois Press, 1977.

Oberbeck, S. K. "Bad Trip." *Newsweek*, 31 July 1972, p. 70.

"*Playboy* Interview: Hunter Thompson." *Playboy*, Nov. 1974, pp. 75–90, 245–46.

Raban, Jonathan. "The New Mongrel." *London Magazine* 13, no. 2 (1973): 96–105.

Salisbury, Harrison E. "Travels through America: The Dark Stain." *Esquire*, Feb. 1976, pp. 43–44.

Seligson, Tom. "The Tripping of the Presidency, 1972." *New York Times Book Review*, 15 July 1973, p. 7.

Vonnegut, Kurt, Jr. "A Political Disease." *Harper's*, July 1973, pp. 92–94.

Woods, Crawford. "The Best Book on the Dope Decade." *New York Times Book Review*, 23 July 1972, pp. 17–18.

Tom Wolfe

PRIMARY

The Kandy-Kolored Tangerine-Flake Streamline Baby. New York: Farrar, Straus and Giroux, 1965; rpt. New York: Pocket Books, 1966.

The Pump House Gang. New York: Farrar, Straus and Giroux, 1968; rpt. New York: Bantam Books, 1969.

The Electric Kool-Aid Acid Test. New York: Farrar, Straus and
   Giroux, 1968; rpt. New York: Bantam Books, 1969.
Radical Chic and Mau-Mauing the Flak Catchers. New York: Farrar,
   Straus and Giroux, 1970; rpt. New York: Bantam Books, 1971.
The New Journalism. Ed. Tom Wolfe and E. W. Johnson. New York:
   Harper and Row, 1973.
The Painted Word. New York: Farrar, Straus and Giroux, 1975; rpt.
   New York: Bantam Books, 1975.
*Mauve Gloves and Madmen, Clutter and Vine and Other Stories,
   Sketches, and Essays.* New York: Farrar, Straus and Giroux, 1976.
The Right Stuff. New York: Farrar, Straus and Giroux, 1979.

SECONDARY

Bellamy, Joe David. "Tom Wolfe: Interviewed by Joe David Bellamy."
   Pp. 75–96 in *The New Fiction: Interviews with Innovative Amer-
   ican Writers.* Urbana: Univ. of Illinois Press, 1974.
Bryan, C. D. B. "The SAME Day: Heeeeeewack!!!" *New York Times
   Book Review*, 18 Aug. 1968, pp. 1–2.
Gray, Paul. "Generation Gaffes." *Time*, 27 Dec. 1976, pp. 62–64.
Hentoff, Margot. "Dr. Pop." *New York Review of Books*, 22 Aug.
   1968, pp. 20–21.
Hoggart, Richard. "The Dance of the Long-Legged Fly: On Tom
   Wolfe's Poise." *Encounter*, Aug. 1966, pp. 60–71.
Kroll, Jack. "Inside the Whale." *Newsweek*, 26 Aug. 1968, p. 84.
Lewin, Leonard C. "Is Fact Necessary? A Sequel to the *Herald Tri-
   bune–New Yorker* Dispute." *Columbia Journalism Review* 4, no. 4
   (1966): 29–34.
Lieber, Joel. "Day-Glo and Light Nights." *Nation*, 23 Sept. 1968, pp.
   282–83.
Macdonald, Dwight. "Parajournalism, or Tom Wolfe and His Magic
   Writing Machine." *New York Review of Books*, 26 Aug. 1965, pp.
   3–4.
————. "Parajournalism II: Wolfe and *The New Yorker*." *New York
   Review of Books*, 3 Feb. 1966, pp. 18–24.
Richardson, Jack. "New Fundamentalist Movement." *New Republic*,
   28 Sept. 1968, pp. 30, 34–35.
Sheed, Wilfrid. "A Fun-House Mirror." *New York Times Book Re-
   view*, 3 Dec. 1972, pp. 2, 10–12.
Tuchman, Mitch. "The Writings of Tom Wolfe: The Manchurian
   Candidate." *New Republic*, 25 Oct. 1975, pp. 21–24.
Wolfe, Tom. "The Author's Story." *New York Times Book Review*, 18
   Aug. 1968, pp. 2, 40–41.

Wood, Michael. "His Job Is to Hide His Opinions." *New York Times Book Review*, 22 July 1973, pp. 20–21.

Michael Herr

PRIMARY

Dispatches. New York: Alfred A. Knopf, 1977.

SECONDARY

DeMott, Benjamin. "Two Reporters: At Peace and War." *Atlantic*, Jan. 1978, pp. 91–93.

Gray, Paul. "Secret History." *Time*, 7 Nov. 1977, pp. 119–20.

Locke, Richard. "Field Reports: Alaska and Vietnam." *New York Times Book Review*, 18 Dec. 1977, pp. 3, 26–27.

Malone, Michael. "Books in Brief: *Dispatches*." *Harper's*, Dec. 1977, pp. 108–9.

Plummer, William. "Ecstasy and Death." *Saturday Review*, 7 Jan. 1978, pp. 36–38.

Prescott, Peter S. "In the Quagmire." *Newsweek*, 19 June 1978, pp. 80–82.

Sale, Roger. "Hurled into Vietnam." *New York Review of Books*, 8 Dec. 1977, pp. 34–35.

Sokolov, Raymond. "Heart of Darkness." *Newsweek*, 14 Nov. 1977, pp. 102–4.

Index